Hear Yourself

PREM RAWAT

HEAR
Yourself

How to Find Peace
in a Noisy World

HarperOne
An Imprint of HarperCollinsPublishers

HarperCollins books may be purchased for educational, business, or sales promotional use. For information, please email the Special Markets Department at SPsales@harpercollins.com.

FIRST EDITION

Designed by Bonni Leon-Berman
Edited by Tim Rich

Library of Congress Cataloging-in-Publication Data has been applied for.

ISBN 978-0-06-307074-5

21 22 23 24 25   LSC   10 9 8 7 6 5 4 3 2 1

CONTENTS

INTRODUCTION

Over the years, I have met and spoken with many people who are on a journey of self-discovery. Some have dedicated their lives to finding enlightenment and are constantly exploring ideas and techniques from around the world. Others have simply wanted to understand themselves a little better, to grow as a person or to experience a greater sense of fulfillment and joy in their life.

Travel with me for part of your journey and you might be surprised where we go. We are heading away from the realm of theories and beliefs toward a unique form of knowledge. To somewhere within you that's free of everyday distractions. To a place where you really can experience clarity, fulfillment, and joy. To a place of inner peace. Our path will take us through mindfulness and heartfulness to peacefulness. Whoever you are, peace is in you—self-knowledge is what enables you to experience it, and this book will show you how.

I find there is a lot of confused intellectual noise around the topic of understanding the self, but the purpose of gaining self-knowledge could hardly be simpler: it's about us experiencing that refreshing clarity, deep fulfillment, and profound, immeasurable joy—and many, many other wonders—by being at one with the universe of peace inside us. This feeling of peace is at the heart of who we truly are.

To be clear: my aim is to help you develop your understanding of peace and what connecting with the peace inside might mean in *your* life, but only *you* can make your journey from outer noise to inner peace. No one can *give* you peace; it's something only you can uncover for yourself, within yourself. As you do so, you come to understand who you are in new ways. There are lots of things that are automatic in our lives—things that happen for us easily—but finding inner peace can take work! Being fully conscious requires effort. As Einstein said, "Wisdom is not a product of schooling, but of the lifelong attempt to acquire it."

As the stories and ideas within this book unfold, I hope you'll get to enjoy unexpected perspectives on something we all share, something I feel we should celebrate much more in our lives: our incredible human spirit. There's also a remarkable character I particularly want you to meet and get to know. But more on that person in a moment.

Many people say they feel challenged by the rising volume of noise going on around them. In our crowded cities and busy, digitally enhanced lives, it's often difficult to find time and space for the quiet simplicity of being. "Progress" is reaching ever further into rural areas too, bringing much-needed benefits and opportunities but also new demands on individuals and communities. It's quite a time to be alive, with innovation creating such wonderful possibilities, yet sometimes the noise that accompanies this progress can feel like an unwelcome distraction.

Actually, the noise going on out there is nothing compared

to the noise we often generate within our own minds: the problems and issues we can't seem to solve, the anxieties and self-doubts we can't seem to soothe, the ambitions and expectations we can't seem to satisfy. We may feel irritation, resentment, and even anger toward others, and disappointment with ourselves. Or perhaps we feel we're held back by a lack of focus or a sense of being overwhelmed, by confusion and procrastination, or by the mental acrobatics we perform each day in search of pleasure and security. In this book I will address the impact negative thinking has on us, and set out a way to reach a deeper, unchanging sense of our self that exists *beyond our thoughts*.

A DIFFERENT PATH

How do I know that my approach works? Because it has worked for me, and that's why I have the confidence to share it with you. I was thirsty and I came to a well, and then my thirst was quenched. Are there other approaches? Absolutely. Why didn't I go on and try them out? Because I was no longer thirsty!

You can use my approach to life regardless of your religious, ethical, or political beliefs (or, for that matter, your nationality, class, gender, age, or sexuality). It's not a replacement for what you believe, because it's about *knowing*, not believing—a fundamentally important difference I'll explore further. Knowing can give you a deep, deep connection with the best of your human spirit and enable you to experience your self in all its dimensions. It's up to you to decide how that relates to your beliefs.

You'll find that I invite you to treasure and trust your heart, and to not rely solely on your mind as your guide. The mind shapes much of our day-to-day experience, and it can be incredibly helpful to understand how it behaves (and misbehaves). It's important we recognize the mind's positive and negative effects on our lives, embracing opportunities to enrich our ideas and sharpen our intellect. But too often our societies champion the mind at the expense of the heart. Brainpower can't do everything. For example, I'm not sure our mind alone can provide a satisfying answer to the question "Who are you?" My *mind* has never taken me all the way to the place of inner peace within me. To function properly, our mind relies heavily on everything that is put into it, while the heart draws much more on the DNA of a human being.

Speaking of the mind, I have one request of you as a reader: only accept what I write in this book if you *feel* the truth of it for yourself. Whether your intellect is skeptical or accepting of my message, also open up to what your inner self is saying. Give this approach a fair chance. Rather than telling you what to think, the chapters that follow will present some possibilities for you to consider. I'm not here to convince you with logic, just to share experiences, views, and stories that might provide helpful perspectives. Heartfelt words clearly expressed can act as stepping-stones to understanding, and I offer the words in this book as a pathway through ideas and beyond—to the world of inner experience. Please do measure what I say in your mind, but also listen with your heart.

WHO AM I?

Before we go any further, I should tell you something about me.

I was born in Haridwar, India, in 1957, and grew up in nearby Dehra Dun, in the foothills of the Indian Himalayas. The source of the Ganges River springs from the mountains above the city, and it's considered a sacred pilgrimage area by Hindus. In fact, *Hari dwar* means "door to god." It's not a particularly large place, but every year millions of visitors attend holy festivals there. It's a remarkable thing to witness.

So, I was raised in a place where people have long taken religion very seriously and express their beliefs in powerful and evocative ways. My father, Shri Hans Ji Maharaj, was an eminent speaker on the subject of peace and drew crowds of thousands. From an early age he had traveled the mountains—and later visited many towns and cities—in search of holy men who could provide him with wisdom. He was often left disappointed.

The breakthrough for him came when he met Shri Swarupanand Ji, a Guru* in what was northern India and is

---

* In India, "Gu" means "darkness" and "Ru" stands for "light," so a Guru is someone who can take you from darkness to light. You might think of them as a life guide.

now, following the Partition, Pakistan. My father felt he had at last encountered a true teacher—someone with a profound understanding of the human spirit. This experience truly changed him. He had found what he was looking for: a deep understanding of the self and an almost indescribable sense of inner peace. I saw him weep when he recalled what it felt like to learn from the man he called his "Master." He would often quote a couplet by the fifteenth-century Indian poet Kabir, who had experienced something similar with his own teacher:

I was being swept away in this river of darkness
    —of this world, of society—
  and then my Master handed me a lamp.
He showed me this beautiful place inside me, and now
I am content.

My father and mother finally settled in a house in Dehra Dun, but my father still worked from the center he had established in Haridwar, not far away. From there he began to share his message with whoever wanted to listen. His approach gave expression to an ancient tradition that had been handed down from teachers to students over centuries, and in my father's case, from Shri Swarupanand Ji, who had chosen my father as his successor. The core of my father's message was that the peace you are looking for is not waiting out there in the world; it's already within you—but you must *choose* to connect with it. As you'll see, choice is central to my own approach.

My father refused to follow the conventional line on who was eligible to gain wisdom. Indian society was riven by snobbery, suspicion of foreigners, and a brutal caste system, but my father saw individuals as part of a universal human family. Whatever your race, social background, or gender, you were welcome to join him and listen when he spoke. I remember that at one event he invited an American couple on stage, making them guests of honor and sitting them on chairs. It was a clear challenge to anyone who thought non-Indians were spiritually unclean and the lowest of the low. I share my own feelings about our universal human connections in chapter 11.

I learned from my father whenever I could, often sitting at his feet as he addressed audiences of followers and others seeking insight. I first spoke at one of his events when I was four years old. My message that day was simple: peace is possible when you start with yourself. I had always felt the truth of that in my heart and, despite being so very young, it seemed entirely natural to stand up and share that insight with the people sitting before me.

One day, two years later, I was playing outside with my brothers when a family friend came to us saying, "Your father wants to see you all inside. Now!" We thought, "Uh-oh, what have we done?" When we went inside, father asked us whether we would like to receive Knowledge. That was the word he and others used to describe a set of insights and techniques related to self-knowledge. Without stopping to think, we all said yes.

That session with my father didn't last long, and it was only over the following years that I developed a proper understanding of what he had passed on to me that day, and which I will pass on to you. I realized that I had started to gain a much wider perspective on life, better appreciating that we aren't just shaped by what's outside us or by our thoughts. There's something else going on inside too—something incredibly powerful.

I already had a sense of the inner world, but it was at this particular point that I started to see how self-knowledge was a route to personal peace and that practicing it enabled me to stay centered and grounded. I felt that Knowledge was giving me focus and confidence when others often seemed unsure of themselves. With Knowledge, there's no need to be anywhere else or think of anything else. No need for an awareness of anything other than the sweet delight of just being. And I began to understand that peace is not a luxury in our lives; it's a necessity.

One day, a little while after I was given the techniques of self-knowledge, I was sitting in our garden in Dehra Dun when an extraordinary sense of peace settled inside me. It was then that I first truly understood inner peace is more than a set of passing feelings and that its essence is not attached to the outside world. I talk more about this experience in chapter 3.

FROM THE GANGES TO GLASTONBURY

When I was eight and a half, my father passed away. As you can imagine, that was a terrible shock for me, my mother, my sister, my brothers, and the entire family. It left an enormous hole both in our lives and those of his followers.

My father had sent me to a Roman Catholic school in Dehra Dun—St. Joseph's Academy—so I could learn English. He had hoped that one day I might share his understanding of self-knowledge with people overseas—with all of humanity, in fact. After my father passed, my own life's purpose suddenly became clear to me: I had to continue his work, sharing the message that peace is possible—wherever people might listen, all around the world.

It was a pretty bold ambition for such a young boy, but it felt obvious that's what I needed to do. The only way to start was by addressing my father's followers, so I plucked up enough courage to face the crowds on my own and soon found myself speaking across India. To this day, I am struck by the remarkable character of the Indian people. The country has been through so much—so many conquests and challenges—but has survived through the resilience of the people. I've met so many incredible individuals on my tours around India.

In the 1960s, visitors from the US and Europe arrived in Dehra Dun, often in search of new ideas about life. Some started to come and hear me speak. I talk about my first encounter with these strange visitors later in the book. A group of them listened closely to my message and, after a while, said they wanted to share my teachings with people back home, so they invited me to come to England. I was keen to go, but at just thirteen years old I was expected in class by the teachers at St. Joseph's, so the trip had to be arranged for the school holidays.

Just a few days after arriving in the UK, in June 1971, I found myself driven from London down to the countryside. At the end of our journey, I stepped from the car onto the Pyramid Stage at the Glastonbury music festival. It was only the second Glastonbury, which has now become a world-famous event. That night I talked briefly about the power of self-knowledge and personal peace to a pretty surprised, boisterous crowd. The message seemed to resonate with many of them. My arrival in the UK and this appearance at Glastonbury attracted press attention, and people started to seek me out.

That year I visited and spoke in the US for the first time, and interest began to grow there too. I was meant to go home for the new school term, but I decided to stay away a little longer. I remember calling home to tell my mother that I wasn't planning to go back. I happened to be in Boulder, Colorado, at the time. I reported that great things were happening in the States. That was really the purpose of the trip: to explore whether people abroad were even interested in this message of peace. In India many people were terribly poor, yet they had access to the treasures of self-knowledge. But would the relatively wealthy folk of America and elsewhere feel the need to better connect with their self? It soon became abundantly clear to me that people in the West *did* have the same thirst for self-knowledge and inner peace as people back home.

So, there I was: thirteen years old and many thousands of miles from home, but with a clear sense of the opportunity ahead. And I knew my own mind. After some persuasive arguments from me, my mother agreed—reluctantly—that I should stay a little longer. Neither of us knew it then, but I was soon to establish a new life in the US, addressing increasingly large crowds both there and further afield. And within a few years I was to meet my wife, Marolyn, and start a family in America.

LOOKING IN THE RIGHT PLACE

For a long time now I've been traveling the world with my message of personal peace. When we feel that peace inside us, we start to influence those around us. Peace is beautifully contagious. I've spoken about this everywhere from United Nations meetings to high-security prisons, from countries that have endured recent conflict (including South Africa, Sri Lanka, Colombia, East Timor, and Côte d'Ivoire) to auditoriums and stadiums in many other nations. I've talked with everyone from world leaders to ex–guerrilla fighters, from crowds of 500,000 and television audiences of millions to small groups, and to many people one-on-one. Now I'm speaking to you through this book.

Wherever I go, I want to share that ancient message of

self-knowledge and peace handed down over the years, but I always look to relate the old wisdom to what's going on today. You'll see that although I'm concerned about the personal and social impacts brought by industrial and technological development, I also celebrate the benefits of modernity.

Technology certainly plays a significant role in my day-to-day life. Flying is important to me, for example. When I was young, I always used to think about airplanes and dreamed of being able to fly. I really wanted to be up among the clouds. After I got to America, I decided to train to become a pilot. Since then, flying has enabled me to take control of my traveling and reach far-off places to share my message. Flying has been a hugely rewarding part of my life.

Over the decades that I've been traveling and speaking we've seen an extraordinary rise in living standards around the world. Not everyone in society has benefited, of course, as a trip to India (or to the poorest parts of America) will show you. But the increase in general material prosperity has been remarkable. And yet, wherever I travel, there seems to be no corresponding increase in the number of people who feel content with their circumstances, fully connected with themselves, and clear about their purpose. People often tell me they feel their *self* is missing, but it's not really missing—they're just searching in the wrong place.

It can be tempting to go *out* to the world to find what we're searching for—and that can bring great experiences our way—but true fulfillment is there for us only when we direct our consciousness inward. Peace is perfectly formed within us from the moment we're created, but we can lose touch with it as we meet life's distractions. People look everywhere for self-knowledge and peace, but there's no need to keep searching when you already have what you seek.

We need to truly *feel* who we are. And that's the remarkable character I mentioned earlier who is central to all this, the person you need to know better than anyone else: you. My view is that you have everything you need within you—all the resources required to truly know yourself. Clarity, contentment, and kindness are in you. Darkness is in you, but light is in you too. Even when you are sad, joy is still in you. Those feelings don't come from anywhere else, they are part of you, although you might have lost sight of them. Ultimately, what I do is give you a mirror so you can start seeing your inner self clearly.

WHAT'S YOUR STORY?

My family didn't have television until quite late on, and the radio stations would only broadcast for a few hours a day, but our home was full of storytellers. There is a very long tradition of oral storytelling in India, with teachers passing on tales to students, students sharing them with others, and so on. This conversational approach meant narratives could reflect contemporary concerns and events, so they always felt relevant. The ancient holy Indian scribe Ved Vyās appreciated the spoken tradition but also felt that certain stories were getting lost over time, so he started writing them down. He's now revered as the author of the Sanskrit epic *Mahabharat* and is often credited with writing or compiling other famous collections of Indian texts such as the Vedas and the Puranas. Both spoken and written stories kept everyone in our household entertained, but we also learned from them. Now, as a speaker, I share stories that have resonated with me over the years—including tales from around the globe—and I've included a number of my favorites in this book.

Traditional stories usually begin with "Once upon a time," but the big story I want to tell you starts slightly differently: "Once upon *this* time there lives *you*." You have a story that you have been writing since you were born, and it's important you keep putting yourself at the heart of the action. You need to enjoy who *you* are. If you're not careful, everyone else can become the main characters in the drama of your life—partners, family, friends, colleagues, celebrities, politicians, even strangers—but you have to keep putting *you* at center stage. "Isn't that being self-obsessed?" I hear you ask. Quite the opposite—and I'll tell you why starting with yourself is actually the best thing you can do for other people.

KNOW THYSELF

At some point in human history people began to realize that there's a level of consciousness beyond the thinking necessary for day-to-day survival. We don't know exactly when this understanding emerged. What we do know is that signs of self-knowledge can be traced like a beautiful thread through many of the greatest cultures and civilizations, each adapting it in ways that made sense to them.

Think of those famous words often ascribed to the classical Greek philosopher Socrates: Know thyself! The same phrase was also said to be written in stone at the Temple of Apollo in Delphi. Some historians believe those words may have been adopted by the Greeks from the Ancient Egyptians. The inner temple at Luxor in Egypt was reputed to have an inscription saying: "Man, know thyself, and you are going to know the gods." More on those gods later. The point is that the phrase isn't "know your history" or "know your culture" or "know your society"—it's utterly precise: "know *yourself.*"

Do you know yourself?

When I ask that question, most people simply smile and say something like "perhaps" or "I'm not sure." Who are you? It's a simple question that can be tough to answer, partly because we usually try to respond with words rather than feelings. Words are a good place to start, but knowing our self is really about what we *experience* rather than how we define ourselves. I'm here to tell you that, over many centuries, people have experienced the fulfillment that comes with true self-knowledge—and you can too.

Part of my job is to help counteract the effects of a world that can easily distract you from who you are. Many people will tell you what you are not; I'm here to help you know what you are. Many people will happily tell you everything that's wrong with you; I'm here to help you appreciate everything that's right with you. Many people will be quick to say you should be more like this or that; I'm here to say you have perfection inside you. Along the way you get to answer for yourself "Who am I?" And perhaps even "Why am I here?"

To this day, my message starts with the fundamental truth that peace is in every one of us without exception. This feels like an important statement in the face of so much confusion, cynicism, fear, and despair in our world. You'll find my approach simple, practical, and easy to apply. It's not about studying for years and years—you have what you need inside you right now. But self-knowledge can only truly begin when you take responsibility for your own well-being and choose to explore within. In my experience, peace is only possible when *you* start with *your* self.

The Ancient Greek philosopher Aristotle said: "Knowing yourself is the beginning of all wisdom." From self-knowledge and peace flows a deliciously sweet feeling of joy, clarity, fulfillment, love, resilience, and many other things—sensations that can be enjoyed for themselves and do not have to be attached to anyone or anything else. Just let this thought sit inside you for a moment: you have a lifetime's supply of inner peace that isn't dependent on or defined by other people, or by anything outside you. It is yours and yours alone. It is utterly perfect, and it lives right in your heart. That's where we're now headed.

HEAR THE SECRET SOUND

The fifteenth-century Indian poet Kabir said: "If you want the truth, I'll tell you the truth: listen to the secret sound, the real sound, that is inside you." Self-knowledge is like music—as you start to understand yourself you begin to hear the many beautiful sounds this life can play for you. It's as if your ears are becoming attuned to more and more frequencies. At last, above the noise, you hear yourself. You turn into a musician too, producing wonderful melodies that will delight those able to hear them. And you may well inspire a few harmonies. But, like any musician, you must learn your instrument and practice, practice, practice.

I remember a time, back in Dehra Dun, when people used to perform music in their house, just for the pleasure of it. Very few of them were proper musicians by any stretch of imagination, but they would play on and on, often with the other people and resident animals of the house going about their business around them. Somebody might have had a *dhapli* (a tambourine), and there could have been a little keyboard such as a harmonium, and a one-stringed instrument like a guitar called an *ektara*. Usually the sound was pretty basic, but the players were wonderfully immersed in the experience of playing.

My father would sometimes stand outside to listen. "Shhh!" he would say. "Don't let them know we're standing here, be-cause then they're going to stop playing!" He wanted them to stay in that moment and express themselves without thinking, without worrying about performing for others and striving to be technically correct. That's really very similar to practicing self-knowledge: it's not about the perfection of the instrument used or the audience reaction to the performance; it's about the feeling experienced by the player.

Imagine how the feeling of peace could change the way you live each precious moment. Imagine if everyone around you could gain this deep connection with who they are. Imagine if everyone could hear and play the music of self-knowledge. Think of the impact on individuals, on families, on communities, on politics, on war, on our world.

Well, it starts with one person at a time—in this case, *you*.

Let's begin.

CHAPTER 1

Get Past the Noise
Between Your Ears

Our time is very precious—who knows how much we will have? Each day we receive this fabulous gift of life. The greatest responsibility we have to ourselves is to ensure we live each moment as best we can. When that happens, it's as if life blossoms for us in all its glory. Even in the difficult times we can experience the pure joy of life itself. But to make the most of our time we must take care with our attention, giving it only to what matters—what we really need to do and what most fulfills us. Everything else is noise.

Each day I want my agenda to be clear. The agenda for today is joy. The agenda for today is kindness. The agenda for today is fulfillment. The agenda for today is love. Above all, the agenda for today is to live in peace. Extracurricular activities might appear—all those practical or necessary things that can come into our lives—but none should distract me from the priority of living life to the fullest.

People often talk about the need to focus our attention. My suggestion is that we see most clearly when we are looking both outside and inside ourselves. There are incredible opportunities to be enjoyed in our world, but if we're only engaged with what's going on "out there" and lose touch with what's happening within us, we can lose our perspective and start to feel unbalanced.

When I say "within us," I'm referring to the deepest part of who we are. I think of this as the heart rather than the mind. Too easily we can end up spending all of our time in the restless world of the mind—the province of thoughts, ideas, expectations, projections, anxieties, criticism, and fantasies about things outside of us—and then one day we ask ourselves: "Is *that* all there is? Is *that* all I am? Am I just a vehicle for these ever-flowing thoughts?" This thirst for a sense of personal meaning and completeness beyond what goes on in our mind transcends culture.

Well, *is* that all there is? *Is* that all we are? *Are* we much more than a mind within a body? The answer is that there's much more—much, much, much more—to life and to us than what passes through our head. Indeed, it's often our mind that keeps us distracted from a deeper connection to our self. The challenge for many people is that they grew up surrounded by external distractions but were never shown how to connect inside *beyond thinking*.

Without that deeper connection within, we may well feel that a part of us is missing—perhaps the most important part—but we don't quite know what's absent, or where to find it. What's missing is a connection with our own sense of inner peace, with the heart of who we are. When we are connected with peace, our experience of life is enriched by clarity, by a clear sense of what *really* matters. When each day we start from a place of calm—of truly knowing our self—then we can go out into the external world focused on what we most want to do, experience, and feel.

So, peace, fulfillment, and many other wonders are available to us, but we need to make sure we're looking in the right place. Before we head there, it might help to understand a little more about this thing called noise.

THE BUSYNESS OF LIFE

Perhaps you can relate to this: You wake from sleep, slowly open your eyes, yawn, and stretch. And immediately, they jump on you. All those thoughts about the day ahead. All those goals you have to achieve and plans you must pursue. All those expectations and opinions from family, friends, and colleagues. All those problems at home or at work. All those concerns about things that happened yesterday or might happen tomorrow. The past and the future are coming together in a cacophony of noise.

It's as if the many distractions in your world were sitting patiently at the end of the bed waiting for you to emerge from slumber. And now they've leaped into life. *Your* life. In fact, sometimes the distractions are so impatient, they just come and wake you up way too early in the day. "Time to get up!" they cry. "We need to be fed!"

I hear a chorus of complaint from some of my friends:

"There are so many demands on my time!"

"I don't get a minute to myself!"

"It never stops!"

People often speak like they've become servants to the business—the *bus*yness—of life. All too easily we can let distractions set our agenda, and then time seems to melt into thin air. When that happens, we can miss the blessings of our waking hours—the contentment and joy that are there for us to savor. This is how noise can detract from our experience of life.

THE WONDERS AND CHALLENGES OF TECHNOLOGY

Technology was going to help us solve the problem of busyness. We were told it would take away the boring, time-consuming tasks and leave us free to do more of what we love. It hasn't quite worked out like that.

Now, I like technology, so don't mistake this for a suggestion that we should go back to a less technically advanced way of life. Invention and innovation have done amazing things for humankind in my lifetime, including for me. Technological progress has helped raise levels of prosperity, health, and comfort for many millions of us. It has enabled us to travel farther, faster, and safer than ever before. It has allowed us to stay in touch with loved ones who live many miles away. It has brought new services, information, and entertainment into our homes. And I hope there's much more to come, particularly for the poorest people on our planet.

My own experience of technological change started when my parents bought a refrigerator. Back then, India was really lagging behind in terms of technical progress, so when this expensive object arrived in our household, we were all a bit in awe. It was placed in a room separate from the kitchen, and we didn't really know what to put in it. For a while it just held jugs of cold water, then someone said: "Come on, you can store all your vegetables and fruit!" And they showed us what it could do.

I was filled with curiosity as a kid, and I really wanted to know whether the light inside the refrigerator went out when the door was closed. So I got in it, then closed the door. About two minutes later, someone came and opened it. They were shocked—there's something alive inside this refrigerator! But hey, I had my answer.

Then the telephone arrived. But rather than punching in a number, we used to lift the receiver and the operator would be there, waiting to connect us. If it was a local call, we'd just give the name, and they would put us through.

Later, when we visited Delhi, we would use a telephone to find out whether a family friend, who owned one of the first TVs in the city, was going to turn his set on that evening. We always wanted to go and watch it with him! What an incredible journey from there to viewing the latest movie on your tablet or phone.

We can appreciate the benefits of technology and embrace innovation, but along with the wonders come challenges. We must take care to ensure technology always works for our benefit. When it feels like technology is starting to run me, I don't like it. I want to keep control and make the decisions that affect me. I want to be the one who turns the technology off and on.

IT WILL PASS

I sometimes find the emotional connection people form with their devices rather surprising. I was in Cambodia a few years ago giving a talk to some great students. At one point during questions, a young woman stood up, looking pretty upset. "I have watched your videos," she said, "and you said that we should not live with the past, we should live with the present . . ." Well, immediately I started to imagine that she must have gone through something traumatic—perhaps the death of her parents—and I was already feeling pretty happy that she was opening up about this to me. And then she said: "So, yesterday I lost my phone. And I still regret this and I feel sorry. What can I do to make myself happy again?"

I hadn't expected something so lacking in tragedy, yet the young woman seemed genuinely sad. I replied to her like this: "Were you born with a phone? No. You cannot judge the moments of your life by a phone. To live, do you need a phone? Do you know how long civilization existed before there was a phone? For thousands and thousands of years people didn't have phones. So, were they all sad? No! Things will come and go. Your joy cannot be attached to those things. Should you be concerned? Yes. Should you be sad? No!

"When the wind blows really hard, the trees that don't know how to bend break. But the trees that know how to sway with the wind, they stay. It's just a storm; it will pass. But *you* have to be above it. You will be okay."

ALWAYS ON

So, I can see that technological progress is positively transforming the world around us in many ways, and I'm delighted about that. It's when it comes to the world inside us that my feelings become a little more complicated.

Technology—especially in communications—can be an amplifier of the noise in our lives, a multiplier of the distractions that compete for our attention. Many people report that they feel bombarded by e-mails, texts, notifications, posts, and so on. But we also worry about the messages we *haven't* yet received and the people who *don't* yet follow us.

Humans can adapt very quickly to new situations, but it

feels as if some of us are being carried along by the tide of innovation rather than navigating our own course. Technology is there to help us keep in touch with each other, but it can feel like we're losing touch with ourselves instead. Sometimes it seems as if our devices are weighing us down. It's like we've bought a horse to get us from one place to another, but we've ended up carrying the horse!

When we feel the demands of the technology calling us, we should ask ourselves: In this moment, do I feel free or have I surrendered a part of myself to this constant connectivity? We're told it's an "always on" world—might it benefit us to press pause more often?

One challenge is that new forms of social media present an ever-flowing river of new material. This can be exciting and rewarding, but instead of being refreshed by what's new, we can end up always wanting what's next. Then we become anxious about possibly missing something important. There's an acronym for this feeling: FOMO—fear of missing out.

Now we see a new wave of technology coming into our lives, too: innovations that might do great things for us, but with consequences we need to consider carefully. Artificial intelligence, augmented reality, virtual reality: there are lots of exciting possibilities, but we must ensure the technology helps make our day-to-day reality better. I'm reminded of a comment made by the economist John Kenneth Galbraith: "The drive toward complex technical achievement offers a clue to why the US is good at space gadgetry and bad at slum problems."

I'm sometimes asked: "What's going to happen when artificial intelligence comes?" Well, you will still be you. I will
still be me. Human beings will still be human beings. It may
amuse you to learn that whenever they require some mainte-
nance, I use a 2.6-billion-year-old sharp-edged stone to get the
back off my digital devices. Some technologies retain their
value.

The great science fiction writer and academic Isaac Asimov
said: "The saddest aspect of life right now is that science gathers knowledge faster than society gathers wisdom." But we
always have the opportunity to change that. And we always
need to remember that there is a reality deep within us that
is full of wisdom.

DELIGHT IS MISSING

Our sense of overload is about more than technology, of
course. Sometimes the expectations other people place on
us can add to the pressure we feel. And then there are our
own expectations: the unmet desires and drives, those per-
sistent *wants* that we can never quite shake off. Ambition is
good, but not when it stops us experiencing the full richness
of life. Some of us are so busy trying to be successful that
we don't get time to enjoy who we already are. And some
of us are so busy trying to get somewhere that we don't see
where we are right now. It can be an "always on" world in
our minds, too.

Each generation tries to find ways to respond to that insatiable desire for something else. The Roman philosopher Seneca seemed to understand FOMO. In his essay *On the Shortness of Life* he wrote:

> Men travel far and wide, wandering along foreign shores and making trial by land and sea of their restlessness, which always hates what is around it. "Let's now go to Campania" they say. Then when they get bored with luxury—"Let's visit uncultivated areas; let's explore the woodlands of Bruttium and Lucania." And yet amid the wilds some delight is missing . . . They make one journey after another and change spectacle for spectacle. As Lucretius says, "Thus each man ever flees himself." But to what end, if he does not escape himself?

Some delight is also missing amid the wilds of modern life. The outside world presents wonderful opportunities for us to connect with people and experience new things. Communications technology hugely extends all this, and that's great. But what we're really looking for is inside us. I want to know this of a person: What is the world of social media *inside* you like? Do you *Follow* you? Do you *Like* you? Do you know how to be your own *Friend*? If you can't be a friend to yourself, can you really be a friend to anyone else?

Sometimes we just need to put down our device and sit with the person who is our number one fan—us. As the ancient Chinese philosopher Lao Tzu remarked, "It is good intelligence to know your friends, but it is true wisdom to know yourself."

NOW FOR SOME GOOD NEWS

So, you want to find a better balance between what's going out there in the world and what's happening inside? Reduce the distractions in your life and find contentment? Experience that sweet feeling of being joyful and complete in the moment? Turn down the volume on the noise and hear yourself? This is all perfectly possible. First, however, we need to recognize that the noise in the outside world is irrelevant to feeling peace within. In other words, we only have to deal with the noise between our ears.

People try all sorts of things to escape the noise. They go under the blankets and put pillows over their ears. They climb mountains, they walk in forests, they run. They go up to 30,000 feet and deep down beneath the waves. They go on a pilgrimage and visit silent retreats in remote corners. They go to the temple or church or mosque or shopping mall or bar or street pusher. But the noise is still there. It's stuck *between* their ears, so there's nowhere else it can live. As the American writer Ralph Waldo Emerson put it,

> Though we travel the world over to find the beautiful,
> We must carry it with us or we find it not.

Thus each man or woman always flees their self—but to what end, if they do not escape it? Unless we find the peace within, the noise will always find us.

Now for that good news!

The noise isn't just happening to us; we're *allowing* it to happen to us. We can *choose* when to switch off our devices. We can *choose* how to manage our mental inbox. We can *choose* who we listen to, care about, and respond to.

I mentioned that people try to escape the noise at 30,000 feet. Let me take you up there for a moment. Being a pilot, I've been inside plenty of cockpits and flown different types of aircraft. There's a lot of automation now, with computers making many of the decisions. In fact, as technology has improved, pilots have moved from taking care of the aircraft to taking care of the technology that often flies the plane for them. Ultimately, however, it is a human who flies the plane, not the computer, especially in an emergency. When I was training, my instructors often said to me: "If there's a problem with the technology, just turn it all off and do what you have always done—fly the airplane!"

That's what we need to do when the noise gets too loud in our life: turn off the other stuff and fly your self. And we do that through the choices we make.

Just a moment of positive choosing can be the start of a life-changing journey through self-knowledge to inner calm, focus, contentment, and peace. We head toward inner peace when we choose—*we choose*—to also turn our attention inward. Once we fully connect with our inner self, the noise stops being an intruder and starts to be our friend— just a particularly busy, loud, lively friend we only see when it suits us.

It's important to note the "also" in that phrase "to also turn your attention inwards." It needn't be an either/or choice between technology and inner peace, between noise and contentment, between the outside and inside worlds. People sometimes assume that they can either have all the benefits of modernity *or* inner peace, as if one thing is incompatible with the other. We don't have to sacrifice one for the other; we just have to make sure it's we who are choosing where our attention goes.

THE GANG OF THIEVES

Let's put this approach of positive choosing into action on a particular issue. We are having our time stolen from us: that's what many people seem to feel. Is that true? Perhaps some of the new social media technologies are attention thieves (a few seem to be designed that way), and deep down we all know that our desires can distract us from contentment.

But who opens the door to these thieves? We do! *We* bring the outside world into ourselves. Often, it's exciting and rewarding to encounter new things, people, and information—that's part of learning, after all. But we have to stay in charge of the doorway to our mind and our heart. When we allow just anyone and anything in, we become an accomplice to the theft of our own time. Other people may be catalysts, but we are the main source of our agitation. We are the main source of our confusion. We are the main source of our discontent. We are the main source of our distraction. But we are also the main source of all the powerfully positive qualities that can take us back toward joy, clarity, fulfillment, focus, and inner peace.

When we are always looking for what's next, when what makes us human starts to disappear, when we start relying on something so much that we lose touch with ourselves: that's when we need to temporarily close the door to the outside world and reconnect inside. That's where we find our true freedom.

Getting back in charge of oneself in this way can feel tremendously liberating. It helps us find, appreciate, and fully *be* the person who is living and breathing right here and now. We always have the option to let the noise of the world do its thing and focus our attention inside. I'm the only one who can do this for me; you are the only one who can do this for you. Nobody else has access to your volume control.

Noise begets noise. People mask noise with more noise, and on it goes, getting louder. But there's one thing that conquers the noise: the silence within you. Here are some words from the thirteenth-century poet Rumi:

> You are song, a wished-for song.
> Go through the ear to the center,
> Where the sky is, where wind,
> Where silent knowing.

When we quiet the noise of the mind, the heart can be heard. Then we begin to encounter a very sweet and gentle voice: a calling, not in words but in feeling. What is that feeling? It's the inner expression of "I am, I am, I am." This song of the heart invites us to fully rise to the occasion, and the occasion is none other than life itself.

CLARITY AND ACTION

You might be thinking: that's all very well, but what about when things *demand* my attention? When the noise of life cannot be ignored? Yes, there are always matters we really do need to address, but there are also many day-to-day concerns that go into our negative imagination and get supersized beyond their importance. Just think back to that Cambodian girl and her lost phone. It turned her world upside down, but it was really just a passing moment. It was no big deal, but together all the "no big deals" can add up to the sum of our life.

When we experience pain and suffering, we look for explanations, yet looking for explanations can become a problem too. Rather than try to explain, the first thing I do in the face of a serious problem is turn inside and recognize the most important fact for me: "I am. I am. I am." That gives me the biggest and best perspective from which to view whatever problem has appeared. Self-knowledge starts with understanding that you've got the single most important thing absolutely right—you are alive. You are here, breathing, with all the possibilities that offers. Congratulations!

When problems come at us—which they surely will—we

can always choose to see them for what they are, address them directly, or maneuver around them and move on. As a pilot, you might be sitting in the cockpit and everything is going smoothly until you hit some clear air turbulence. You don't see it—you feel it. It usually starts slowly, and often it just leaves of its own accord. But sometimes it gets worse and you need to act. It's time to leave that altitude and find some better air. Go up, go down, go left, go right, whatever. It's the same with thunderstorms, but the advantage there is that you can see them ahead.

In our everyday life there are always going to be turbulent moments, and sometimes we're going to see them coming and sometimes we're not. That's when we have to choose: either I'm not going to worry about this, or I'm going to take myself to a different altitude. Either choice is better than flying on through the turbulence without deciding one way or another, because then it gets uncomfortable. When that happens, we forget about everything but the turbulence when we could be enjoying the journey. We forget the beautiful views out of the windows. And we stop talking to our fellow passengers.

In the midst of problems we can draw inspiration from the lotus flower. It can thrive even when its roots are in dirty water. However filthy its setting, the flower always looks beautiful. When we feel beset by challenges, we can choose not to let the dirty water of our circumstances stop us from expressing the joy of simply *being*.

WHAT IF?

Regret about the past and anxiety about the future—it becomes tough to flourish in life if we allow ourselves to keep getting caught between these two. Memories nag at us. Worries about tomorrow haunt us. What if that hadn't happened? What if this happens? Our negative imagination gets us both ways. Some people can't bear to think about the past, so they keep looking to the apparent safety of the future. Others live in a fantasy world of nostalgia about yesterday because they fear tomorrow. What if? What if? What if?

Sparta was one of the leading city-states in ancient Greece and its people were famed for being very tough. Having invaded southern Greece and taken other important cities, King Philip II of Macedonia turned his attention to Sparta. An account by the Greek writer Plutarch tells us that Philip sent the Spartans a message asking whether he should come as friend or foe.

"Neither," they replied.

So Philip sent another message: "I advise you to submit without further delay, for if I bring my army into your land I will destroy your farms, slay your people and raze your city."

Once more, the Spartans replied with just one word: "If."

Philip never did attempt to capture Sparta.

What if? What if? What if? Maybe, on this point, we should take the Spartan approach and call out our fear. We too can live a life shaped by our negative imagination and the misshapen illusions it projects onto reality.

Here's a story about illusions and the effect they can have on us.

Once there was a Queen, and she owned a stunning necklace. One day, she was on the balcony, drying her hair, when she took off the necklace and put it on a hook. A crow was flying by, saw the jewelry glinting in the sun, scooped it up, and flew away. Before he got too far, the crow dropped the necklace in a tree and it got caught on one of the branches, above a polluted river.

When the Queen reached for her necklace and found it missing, she threw a tantrum. "Who stole it?" she cried. She had everybody searching, but nobody could find it. She said to the King: "If I don't find my necklace I'm never going to eat again."

The King was deeply concerned and sent his army and others to look for the necklace, but it couldn't be found. So the King finally made an announcement: "Whoever finds the necklace gets half of my kingdom." Then people *really* started looking.

Next day a general walked by the tree and thought he saw the necklace in the river below. He immediately jumped into the dirty water because he wanted half the kingdom. The minister saw the general jumping in, and he too thought he saw the necklace and leaped in. The King saw his general *and* his minister looking in the river and jumped in. By then, more soldiers and villagers had come, and they all got into the water too.

Finally, somebody with a little wisdom said: "What are you doing? The necklace is not down there; it's up there in the tree. You're jumping in after the reflection." So the king said: "Since you found the necklace, half my kingdom is yours." And the wise person said: "Thank you, but I'm happy as I am."

We jump toward our illusions. The greatest illusion is that the distractions in our life are what we seek, yet inner reality offers us more wonder than we could ever hope to see. We always have the possibility to connect with *that* reality.

MIRROR, MIRROR

All our life is lived in today. Right now. This second. And this second. And this second. We can't live in yesterday, we can't live in tomorrow. Besides, today is where the magic happens. Today is the place we can truly feel peace, joy, and love. It's where we should be: present in the present. To experience today, we need to remove yesterday and tomorrow, and then we're left with what's real. The only FOMO we should be concerned about is missing out on reality while we're alive.

Today is a mirror. It reflects us perfectly. It is true and fair, and it portrays not just our face, hair, and clothes but everything about us. It reflects our clarity or confusion. It reflects our confidence or uncertainty. It reflects our kindness or anger.

If you were to stand in front of a mirror, what would you see? Who would you see? What does your reflection represent to you? Are you seeing yourself through your own eyes? You see that your appearance has changed over the years, but can you sense something about you that has never changed?

AT THE CENTER OF YOUR WORLD

We are born with peace in our heart and it is always there in us, at the center of our world. Despite our difficulties and distractions, despite our problems and confusion, peace is possible inside every one of us.

Whatever has happened in our life, there is always that opportunity to reunite all the elements that make us whole. As our outward life becomes busier and more demanding, we can lose touch with what's most important. But everything outside us will come and go, it's just passing by. Take away the noise in your life and the only thing left is you. *You*—deep in your heart—are the constant.

There are different paths to connecting with peace, but just one direction of travel: within. Some people spend their entire life in a perpetual spiritual search engine, going off to visit every corner of what's *out there* in the hope it will give them the big answer *in here*. My advice is stop searching. Peace is not an idea. It's not a theory. It's not a formula. It's not something to be discovered from a passage written in the pages of an ancient book, hidden on a secret shelf in a strange building in an obscure place up a mountain shrouded in mist. Peace is in people, not in things. It is in *you*. And it is there to be sensed, felt, experienced, treasured, and celebrated. The Indian poet Kabir put it like this:

> Be quiet in your mind, quiet in your senses, and also quiet in your body. Then, when all these are quiet, don't do anything. In that state truth will reveal itself to you.

The process of attaining self-knowledge and revealing the peace within is simple, but it's not necessarily easy. Some might gain clarity in a moment; others may try for a lifetime. Over the following pages we'll further explore what finding peace involves and the wonderful treasures it can bring. But first we need to consider why all this matters so very much. And what is this thing called life, anyway?

CHAPTER 2

Discover Your Inner Rhythm

There is a power that has run through the universe for billions of years. It was there before us and it will outlive us. It permeates every atom, and it has brought to life something wonderful called Nature, which includes all that humans create.

Everything that we see, touch, hear, smell, and taste is an expression of this power. It is in the mountains and the valleys, and deep in the caverns below. It is in the forests and the jungles, and in every grain of sand in the deserts and on the beaches. It is in the vast oceans, the lakes and the ponds, and in the roaring rivers, waterfalls, and gentle brooks. It is in the rain, mist, and fog, in the ice and the snow, in every ray of sunshine and every blast of wind. And it is in every city, town, village, and home. It is in all that we breathe, eat, and drink. It is in us and around us—it is *everywhere*.

This is how I understand the life force connecting all living things. Some people call this power God; others may use a different name. For me, it makes no difference which word we attach to this power; it simply *is*.

THE MIRACLE OF YOU

The power manifests in many forms, from cosmic dust—the tiny building blocks of our universe—to countless species, all of them evolving, reproducing, adapting. Imagine the scale of our own transformation, from single-cell organisms in the ocean to creatures walking on land then walking on the Moon.

For a moment, try to imagine every living thing that has existed on Earth. Picture the scale and breadth of that life over many millions of years. Think of the incredible array of animals and plants that have lived. It's estimated there are more trees on this planet right now than stars in our galaxy—more than three trillion of them, according to a study published in *Nature* magazine. That's just today. Think of the trillions and trillions and trillions of trees that have come and gone since Earth took shape.

Think of the wild roses that have come and gone, the insects that have come and gone, the mountains and the waves that have come and gone, the people that have come and gone. Think of the scale of that body of creation that went before us, then understand that it has all led to you—to this moment of your presence here as a living, breathing expression of the universal power. That energy rippling through the universe is now coming through you in the form of breath, making it possible for you to *be*. Here you are, surfing this wave of incredible creativity. This moment has been billions of years in the making.

Can you sense yourself within the great flow of energy that started way back and will continue until who knows when? You are part of the pulsating rhythm of Nature as it's giving life, taking life, giving life, taking life. One seed falls and a tree will grow. Another seed falls and it will become food. Another seed falls and it will rot. Appreciate for a moment Nature's beautiful indifference to anything but the irrepressible acts of creating and destroying.

Somewhere, right now, stars are exploding with unimaginable force. Here on Earth, people are being born. And then there's you, in this ever-expanding, ever-changing universe—experiencing the perfection of *being*.

YOU ARE A WALKING
SUCCESS STORY

The power of the universe has momentarily held apart the past and the future to create now—this narrow slice of time in which all action takes place. This is where we exist. This is where everything exists. What problem or expectation could be so significant in our lives that we might let it distract us from experiencing the flawless beauty of now?

Every time you see a tree, a flower, a blade of grass—it's

what worked. It survived infancy, it grew, it bloomed, it lives. And you too are testimony to this miracle called life. You are a walking success story. What an incredible thing a human being is. We should celebrate ourselves!

Some say we are just the accidents or consequences of evolution. After all, we are 99 percent made up of oxygen, hydrogen, carbon, calcium, nitrogen, and phosphorus. If we mixed those elements in a bottle, added 0.85 percent more potassium, sulfur, sodium, chlorine, and magnesium, and then added the final 0.15 of lesser elements—would that give us a human being? Well, that may describe our bodies, but are we nothing more? Could you fall in love with the contents of that bottle? Could you talk to that bottle of elements about beauty and family and kindness? Could they appreciate the wonder of their existence?

We are far more than the sum of our physical elements, not least because we can consciously connect with our self and all living things around us. Every moment offers us the opportunity to understand and express our gratitude for life. Whether we choose to *take* that opportunity is another matter.

THE EXQUISITE RHYTHM
OF OUR BREATH

Human beings who look for a miracle to explain our purpose have forgotten that it occurs every day in their own life: they breathe. We are born, and the human drama plays out around us and inside us. With each breath we get the opportunity to choose our role and play our part, writing the story of our life.

There is a lot of noise in the world, but there is also a song being sung: the lifelong song of the breath coming in and going out. There are a lot of rhythms in the world, and they are often out of sync with each other, but there is one rhythm that is perfectly in sync with *you*: the lifelong rhythm of the breath coming in and going out. Every breath that moves through us is a blessing, coming in and going out.

The day you were born, everyone in the room was focusing on just one thing, and it wasn't whether you were a boy or a girl. Only one thing: Are you breathing? If you're not, the doctors will do everything they can to ensure the breath of life flows into you. How comforting it is for a new mother to hear their baby breathing. How comforting that the rhythm of their infant's breath is whispering again and again: "All is well, all is well, all is well."

At the other end of the journey, when you're back in the hospital, how do they figure out that you've gone? They check if you're breathing. And they also have this amazing machine that tells them whether you're alive or not. So, what happens if the machine declares you're no longer living but they can see that you're still breathing? Is the doctor going to slap you or the machine? Well, she's not going to come to you and say, "You're dead!" Breath is life.

Here is a couplet from the sixteenth-century Hindu saint and poet Tulsidas:

This body is the vessel to get across the ocean of confusion.
The coming and going of the breath is my blessing.

In my imagination, I see myself on that ocean, putting up my sail to get across. I *choose* to put up my sail. The waves are the waves of good and bad, of right and wrong, of everything that change brings to us. They are the waves of love and disgust, of hope and disappointment, of regret and anxiety. We must sail ourselves across all this, and what we require to accomplish our journey is already within us. You just need to put up your sail and find the wind that is blowing for you, ready to take you across choppy waters to the tranquil seas beyond, to the seas of clarity.

In our lives, we become lost on the sea of confusion when we are mesmerized by, to use a Hindi term, "Maya"—the illusion that what exists and changes in the outside world and within our brain is our true reality. But ultimately, our reality lies deep within us. Wisdom is knowing this.

The flower mantis is an insect that can take the form of the flower on which it is sitting. Another insect passing by sees a flower, not a dangerous mantis. In the moment of realization, when the mantis moves and reveals itself, the prey becomes wise. But how often do *we* see what life truly is? Even if we glimpse the truth, do we not simply return to the illusion— like the insect seeing only a flower? How much of our life is spent believing in "Maya"? And yet the coming and going of our breath is the blessing that points us toward reality—in every inhalation and exhalation.

It seems people have long felt a connection between breath and a sense of our inner self—something more than our physical elements. For example, the Hebrew word *ruah* also means "spirit," "breath," and "wind," and it appears often in the Old Testament of the Bible. You can find more words that combine these and similar meanings in other languages and religious works. One particular example—and its evolving meaning—tells us something significant about how we can lose sight of what's most important. The earliest forms of the term "psyche" were originally a fusion of words meaning "life" and "breath," but "psyche" also came to mean "soul, spirit, and self." In recent times, however, the term "psyche" has been linked closely to the mind—think of "psychology"—and few now associate it with breath. In the same way, today we give a great deal of attention to our thinking and quite easily forget our *breathing*. We can end up embracing the complexity of our minds while neglecting the vital simplicity of our breath.

CELEBRATE EACH BREATH

The arrival of breath in our life is not conditional. Day after day it comes to us without making an appointment, without passing judgment. It comes when we have been good and bad. It comes when we don't think about it and when we do think about it. There is no more valuable thing for you and me. No money can buy the ability to breathe, so how rich does that make us? We are in possession of something priceless.

This gift of breath: we should accept it, understand it, cherish it. And we must also recognize when the noise of life—especially all those thoughts flying around in our head—distracts us from the beauty of the rhythm of life, coming in and going out. For example, regret and anxiety can fog our clarity. What is clarity? It's the clear appreciation that we're blessed with existence.

The opposite of clarity is confusion, and one of the most potent sources of confusion is worrying. Let's think about language again. The historical root of the word "worry" comes from the Old English word "wyrgan," which originally meant "to strangle." Later the sense evolved to mean "seize by the throat and tear," like wolves *worrying* prey. Fear gets us right by the throat—that point in our body where air flows into us. We can worry away our joy of life when we should be celebrating it with each breath. Bring in clarity—and, once again, we start to embrace life, just as life embraces us.

START MAKING WISHES

There are those of us who value each moment but are easily distracted by fear, and then there are those who never really notice that they *are* breathing. In their case, existence has become an automatic assumption. Life has been delegated to the autopilot. When you have lost touch with yourself, you have lost touch with reality.

Often it takes a mortal threat to draw our attention to the preciousness of life. Tell someone they have a week to live, and suddenly the value they place on each breath increases. Instead of waiting for a crisis to show us the gift, perhaps we should follow the advice of the Roman emperor and philosopher Marcus Aurelius: "Do everything as if it is the last thing you will do in this life."

Think of the story of Aladdin and his lamp. When he rubs the lamp, a powerful genie comes and grants him wishes. Imagine that I give you Aladdin's lamp and say: "For two hours this lamp is yours. Go for it: you can wish for whatever you want for those two hours. But, after that, the lamp is mine." What would you do? Would you think: "Oh, I can only have the lamp for two hours, that's so sad. If I could only have it for two and a half hours, I could do so much more. Or three hours. And I should really just finish that other thing I have to do before I start making wishes. To be honest, it's not the most convenient time to be given the lamp. Could I get the lamp next Wednesday instead?"

The lamp is your life. Stop wasting precious time and start rubbing that lamp! Make your wishes, one after another. Grab the opportunity of life and keep that genie as busy as you can for as long as you can.

Here's a story about responding to opportunity. Once there

was a man who made his livelihood selling junk metal. He did very, very well at this, but he was a miser. In fact, he was so miserly he had even sold his own metal possessions and replaced them with poor ones made of wood, stone, and paper. There was no metal in his house.

Out of the blue, a man appeared at his door and said: "See this piece of stone? It will turn any piece of old metal into gold. You are free to use it as you wish, but I will return in a week to take it back."

The metal dealer remembered that he had sold every scrap of metal and needed to buy more. So, as soon as the man had left, he called up the market and asked for the price of scrap metal and the price of gold. Gold was much more valuable than scrap, of course, but he thought the price of scrap was too high. "Hmmm," he thought, "I have all week: I'll wait."

And all week he did wait. Every time he called and got the price of scrap, it was way too high for him. Even when the price started to fall, he felt it was too much. Day after day he put off buying the base metal he needed. There was no way he was going to pay that amount for old metal. And then, exactly one week on, the man appeared at his door.

"I have come for my stone," he said.

The metal dealer was shocked: he had lost all sense of time and hadn't used the stone even once. In desperation, he ran around his house looking for metal objects, but everything he picked up was wood, stone, or paper. Suddenly, the man appeared at his side and took the stone from his hands.

"Time's up," the man said.

BETWEEN TWO WALLS

The number 25,550—do you know what that represents? It's how many days we would get if we lived for 70 years. Not a lot, is it? Even if you live to 100, that's only 36,500 days. Pretty sobering, right?

Now we need to do another sum: subtract all the days that you've already lived. How's your current account looking? (I've done my calculation and I've decided to stop counting!)

Even if things go to plan and you live a full life, time is precious. And then we need to factor in uncertainty, because none of us really know for sure how much credit we have at the bank of life.

We know for sure that there was one day when you arrived in this world and there will be another day when you leave. You can't change that, but *every* day between those two points you can change what you feel and what you experience of this world. That's how to be fully alive. Understand that every single day it's up to you to enjoy the time you have. (And try not to complain too much about taxes.)

Here's one way to think about your existence: you came into life through a door in one wall and you will leave through a door in another. Some people are fascinated by what's on the other side of the second wall; I'm fascinated by what's between the walls.

You can ask those on the other side to describe what it's like, but—in my experience, at least—no one ever calls back. Not even Houdini. The great escape artist had promised his wife he would send her a coded message from beyond the grave, but it looks like even he couldn't escape the finality of death.

So, what happens in the absence of communication from that side of the second wall? We speculate: "The afterlife is like this" or "Heaven is like that" . . . And so we try to create pictures of something that is beyond our imagination.

We don't know whether existence is possible for us over that wall, but we do know one thing for sure: we're here right now, with a chance to accomplish whatever mission feels important to us. For me, that mission is simple: I want to fill my life with joy and I want to share my message that peace is possible, all around the world.

Our life is one long today, not one long yesterday or tomorrow. The present moment is 25,550 days long—or however many days each of us is blessed with. We can learn from the past, but we cannot live there. We can imagine tomorrow, but we cannot live there. The only moment that we can truly experience is now. Now comes one breath at a time. Our life is measured out by our breaths.

Many changes will happen to each of us between coming through the first wall and reaching the second. Whatever takes place—good and bad—it can really help us when we keep recognizing that time is priceless. Perhaps the greatest possible success is to live every moment as fully as we can, even when we face problems. The Roman poet Horace captured this sentiment in the phrase *carpe diem*. It literally means "pluck the day," but it's more commonly expressed as

"seize the day." I like both expressions, but "pluck" also suggests to me the lovely idea of today as a flower that's blooming
and ready for us to savor. It reminds me of some well-known
lines by the seventeenth-century British poet Robert Herrick:

Gather ye rosebuds while ye may,
Old time is still a-flying;
And this same flower that smiles today
Tomorrow will be dying.

There's the beautiful thread of self-knowledge lightly wo-
ven through history, expressed in words that resonate with us
some 375 years later.

LET YOUR LIFE BLOSSOM

Sometimes we are distracted by thinking about tomorrow
and yesterday and fail to grasp the moment. At other times
we might feel that today offers us very little—that there are
no beautiful rosebuds to gather. Many people live in this spirit
of disappointment.

While life can sometimes feel like a barren desert, the seeds
required to produce a magnificent garden are there, waiting
in the earth for the right conditions to grow. They were in us
from the moment we were born. Our job is to water, water,
water the ground and let in the light of clarity, so we give those
seeds what they need to flourish. And when we do that, the

desert will bloom, and it will burst out in every conceivable color. Peace wants to show itself. Peace wants you to know it is there. Peace wants to blossom.

I'm always struck by how resilient and patient those seeds within us are. They will wait a lifetime for the water and the light to come, always packed with the potential to flower. "I'm ready," they say, "whenever the rain and the sunshine come." And that's what we need to remember: however long we have felt our life is like a desert, we always have that potential to bloom.

LEARNING FROM TREES

Everything in Nature has created a space for itself and a relationship with everything else. It has its purpose and tries to fulfill it. Yet sometimes we seem to forget about *our* purpose and *our* potential to bloom.

Perhaps we have something to learn from trees. Did you know that recent scientific research suggests some trees have a "heartbeat"? They move their branches up and down at night, creating a slow pulse of water that flows through their body. They're master strategists of survival, just as we are. They figure out what they need to do for their species to thrive, packaging their seeds so they prosper. They've been working this routine for many years, which is why there are more than three trillion of them (even though some of our kind are reducing the tree population for cynical ends).

Trees design themselves to tolerate the environment they are in, so they can get on with being successful trees. I've seen places in the mountains where there's a tiny crack in the rock and it seems to be the most unlikely place for a tree to grow, but one has. Right there. It has found what it was looking for and took its opportunity.

Whatever our circumstances, whatever our environment, we need to find a way to let our inner nature fully express itself. No opportunity to do that should be ignored or abandoned; no opportunity should be put off until tomorrow. Even when the ground around us seems fallow, there's an incredible world within that's full of fertile potential. If we can start to get the light of clarity and the water of understanding into our life, our desert will bloom.

BECOMING FULLY AWAKE

Why do we have such problems letting our life bloom? Why does the noise so often drown out the music of life? Because we can forget what's important. The journey to peace begins with the appreciation of the simplest but most important thing we have: our existence. That's the starting point for self-knowledge. We always have that opportunity to express gratitude for this life, giving thanks for each breath rather than wasting our attention.

When was the last time that you were deeply thankful for being alive? I'm not just talking about those funeral thoughts:

you know, you see a hearse and think, "I'm glad that's not me in there." I mean being fully awake to the day and the night, really *feeling* your existence.

A human being can be a celebration of life. How wonderful it is when we're thankful to be alive—thankful for the people we love, thankful for the sunshine and the rain, thankful for the seasons, thankful for the sweet music of our life, thankful for the gift of breath. Without gratitude, life is like a social engagement we don't want to be at: "Hello. Thank you for inviting me. Goodbye." With gratitude, we become the life and soul of this party called life.

AN URGENT REMINDER

So there are the two walls—birth and death—and when we get closer to where we imagine the second wall might be, it looms in our mind. Worrying about death can become a huge, ugly, loud distraction—perhaps the noisiest of all the problems. If we're not careful, we can end up celebrating our birthday once a year but thinking about death every day. And here's a terrible irony: every moment spent being anxious about death is a waste of precious life. We can be so taken by the desire to live forever that we forget to live today.

Try as we might, we can't avoid going through that second wall at some point. Even the cleverest among us—or perhaps I should say, *often* the cleverest among us—get distracted from the natural truth that we are mortal.

There's an old story about this that always amuses me: Once there was a doctor and he was really smart—really, really smart. And everyone told him so. He had spent decades of his life helping people live, but now he felt that Death was drawing close for him and he didn't want to go. So he devised a plan.

He knew Death was only allowed to take one of him, not two. So he made a replica of himself, exact down to the last detail. It was just perfect, and of this he was very proud.

One day, Death walked in—without an appointment, I imagine—and saw two of the doctors, there on the bed. The doctor had felt that fateful day nearing and he had already placed himself right next to his replica. Smart move. It really was an excellent copy, so Death became confused: "I can only take one; who do I take?" he wondered.

He thought for a minute, then said: "Doctor, congratulations! You have done an incredible job of replicating yourself. But you made one mistake."

The doctor was lying there, and Death's words were starting to go around and around in his head. He thought to himself: What mistake? How could I have made a mistake? He's wrong, isn't he?

After some time the doctor just couldn't stand it anymore and blurted out: "But there's no mistake!"

Then Death said: "That! That's the flaw!"

The doctor had been undone by his own arrogance. We aren't perfect beings (sorry if that's news to you) and we can't escape our mortality. Wisdom is recognizing this and ensuring you live each day with your eyes wide open: seeing reality clearly, accepting what is, and taking every opportunity for joy and contentment. *Carpe diem.*

SAILING DOWN THE RIVER

There's a song by Kabir in which he says: "You are just a little boat made out of paper, sailing down the river." They're such astute words, because as you go down the river of life, guess what? The paper is getting soaked and is starting to disintegrate, meaning the boat is losing its form and slowly merging with the water. And so it goes.

In the meantime, you need to know you are free to enjoy this life. Everything is in place for you to be an instrument of whatever purpose you desire and to experience the richness of your existence. It all starts when you make that continuous circle of connection within yourself: from gratitude to peace, from peace to gratitude.

That's how I try to respond to the reality of the second wall: I say "try" because none of us ever has clarity 100 percent of the time. I want to live in a state of fully feeling, sensing every aspect of my inner self and the joy that springs from peace. When I'm in that state, I would be happy if the day went on forever. But I know, at some point, night will come.

I'm not afraid of death. I use it as inspiration to experience the best of each moment, and that gives me a sense of urgency. For me, any other way of being is not good enough: it's not enjoying the common wealth we have all been given. Any other way of living is a compromise.

EVERYTHING IS TEMPORARY

This body will be gone one day—I know that—and when my physical self goes, all my thoughts and experiences will go with it. What will be left? Well, there is nothing in this world that actually belongs to me. Sometimes I might say: "Oh, that belongs to me and this is mine," but it's all temporary. Everything that I call my own will one day not be mine.

This reminds me of a story that I like about the Macedonian ruler and military commander Alexander the Great (even though it is very likely a fabrication). According to the tale, on his deathbed Alexander said: "I have three commands. My physicians alone must carry my coffin. My path to the graveyard must be strewn with gold, silver, and jewels. My hands must be left to dangle from the coffin."

The assembled friends and advisers were confused, so his favorite general stepped forward and asked why these were so important. Alexander replied: "I wish people to know that physicians are ultimately powerless and cannot cure us of death. I wish people to know that a life spent pursuing wealth is a waste of precious time. And I wish people to know that we all come empty-handed into this world and we all leave the same way."

Yes, we all leave the same way. And the only things I truly

own in this life are my peace and self-knowledge. They are my reality. Once this life is over, what will remain of me are the memories in other people's hearts.

You know when you go to somebody's house and you have a marvelous time? Perhaps the food and the setting were just fabulous. But long after you have digested the dinner and forgotten quite what the room looked like, your sense of enjoyment remains. You carry that feeling with you and that is enough.

AN INVITATION TO THE INFINITE

For billions of years you and I were nothing. For billions of years or more into the future we will be nothing again. Our time here is the exception. Our job is to live these minutes, hours, and days in an exceptional way.

My invitation to you is this: dare to experience the timeless today of inner peace. Your life here is finite, but you have the opportunity to transcend that and momentarily connect with the infinite—the joy of pure existence. It's a way of consciously experiencing that universal power I described earlier.

The opportunity is for us, as finite beings, to encounter the infinite. It's into this timeless world of pure experience that we're heading in the next chapter.

CHAPTER 3

Ground Yourself in Infinite Peace

When I was growing up in Dehra Dun, we used to have some magical fall days, just before the first hints of winter, when the skies were so, so blue and the air over the Himalayas was absolutely clear. Each morning there was a sheen of dew on the grass and plants, and first light would illuminate the water in the air so that the drops sparkled like diamonds. Those dewdrops were so very small, but they shone like tiny suns.

As the sun warmed the air, all the dew would evaporate, leaving this fresh morning scene where everything became sharply focused and you could see to infinity in the sky. It felt as if time hardly moved on those days. Slowly, in the afternoon, billowing clouds with bright silvery edges would roll in.

I would often sit in our front yard, beneath two magnolia trees. And we had these sweet peas growing on the walls, each with a lovely little flower, and the scent was so delicate and delicious, with just a hint of lavender. There were also what we called dog flowers—some people know them as snapdragons—and we used to squeeze the heads so it looked like they were opening and closing their mouths and barking at us silently. It felt so good to sit there in that place.

One day I went out into the garden and had this desire to grasp the moment. I remember my heart was entirely open to the day and I was happy walking around inspecting everything growing there. A little later, I was sitting under one of the magnolia trees, looking at the clouds and the flowers, when I had an overpowering sense that whatever created me *also* made these magnolia trees and the perfumed flowers, and put the dew on the lawn, and carried the sun from horizon to horizon, and made those fat clouds float across the blue sky. In that moment, the he or she or it that originally created me said, very softly: "Just feel."

It was a perfect sentiment for a perfect moment. *Just feel.*

From then on I could sit under that magnolia tree and go into a feeling in which I had no wants, no wishes, no inner need to do anything. It felt good just to *be*. Ever since, a voice has continued to say to me: "This day is for you," and it means that day back in the garden just as it means the day I'm living in right now.

STAYING IN THE FEELING

That feeling part of me hasn't changed. It really hasn't. But I recognize that, at times, I've layered many other things on top of the purity of that experience. You probably know what

I mean: "I need to have this, and I need to have that. And it's got to be this way, and it's got to be that way. And I'm this, and I'm that. And next I should do this, and then I should do that."

Sometimes, rather than go out and grasp that fresh new morning, I find myself distracted by issues and concerns. That tells me the problems in my life are in danger of taking over life itself. Yes, even someone who has been speaking about peace since the age of four finds it challenging, at times, to stay connected to the clarity inside. That is how powerful the darkness of noise and ignorance can be.

That day in the garden was *for me*, and I've understood that I must never lose that feeling. I have experienced the deep connection again and again and again. It is my reality—a feeling of perfect peace—and everything else is noise (sometimes enjoyable noise, sometimes distracting noise). Perfection is not only the memory of that moment from childhood but the living experience of being able to *just feel* right now.

PEACE ENCOMPASSES ALL BLESSINGS

I have reflected many times on my experience in the garden. I've come to understand that the peace inside us is not about anything other than itself. It is not there to do a job; it's there to *be*. It is not dependent on external things for its purpose and value; it simply *is*. It's something that's entirely for you and not about or reliant on anyone or anything else. Like the young me sitting under the tree in that perfect moment, it just *is*.

That's what I was connecting with back then and it's what I always want to know in my life. The feeling of peace is the deepest version of me. But it is also part of something more than me, more than all of us. After I die and you die, the possibility of peace will go on living in every atom in the universe. It is infinite. When we *just feel*, we are connecting with that infinite peace.

All the good feelings that flow from inner peace are also an end in themselves. The joy within you is not connected to something else; it is joy itself. The love within you is not dependent on or about someone else; it is pure love. You need clarity to see the world of peace inside you and the world around you, but there is also clarity that is pure clarity—to be felt and enjoyed for what it is, not what it does.

Here is an important point: Peace encompasses every other blessing, but nothing else encompasses peace. There is joy in peace, but joy alone isn't peace. There is kindness in peace, but kindness alone isn't peace. There is clarity in peace, but clarity alone isn't peace. These are just different words to express aspects of the same thing. Peace is a unique and total state of being.

HOW TO SLEEP WITHOUT SLEEPING

Someone once asked my father: "What is it like to go deep inside and connect with peace?" He replied: "It's like going to sleep, without sleeping."

The first time I heard that story I was driving, and I had to pull over to the side of the road. I found it so profound. Imagine being in that state: *like being asleep without sleeping.* That merging of two states into one. Imagine how profoundly refreshing that sleepless sleep can be.

When we take away the need for our innermost self to be about other things, we can experience a tremendous sense of freedom. The weight of attachment lifts from our shoulders. Are we humans capable of experiencing something just for what it is, not for what it enables us to do next? Well, it may run counter to our action-led world, but I think we are. Peace is possible for all of us, but we must choose to experience it, not try to manufacture it.

BLIND TO THE OBVIOUS

Peace is right there in us, but many people never get to feel it. It is everywhere and yet elusive. In that way it's rather like light. Look out of the window and you might see a wall. If you look closer, you'll see the bricks in that wall and even the fine details of the mortar between the bricks. If you have a keen eye, you might also perceive the effects of weather on the brick and the angle of shadow, and the many colors brought out by the sunlight or moonlight or streetlight. And there are also reflections of light onto that wall from other surfaces, each adding a cast to the light that falls on that wall. We see the wall, but we don't see the light, because the light is everywhere.

Natural light isn't there to illuminate the world on our behalf—that's just a wonderful and life-giving benefit of light being light. As with inner peace, we can appreciate the effect of light on the world around us, but we should also appreciate the essence of light as a thing-in-itself.

Sometimes the most wonderful thing we can do is just *be*. Too often the distractions of everyday life take our attention away from experiencing the universe inside us. We go through this life seeing the colors reflected back to us by the world outside without seeing the full spectrum of reality within. It transforms our experience of life when we recognize we live on, and are part of, this radiant ground.

THE TIMELESS TODAY

We look at pictures of ourselves as babies or children, or pictures of our children when they were small, and we think of the years that have passed. When we see old friends, we often ask: "How long has it been?" In those moments we feel the river of time roaring onward to the sea of eternity. It can be startling, and it often brings out feelings of regret or anxiety as we think about the distractions we've allowed to waste our time. And then we return to the busyness of our everyday life.

In those moments—before the tyrannies of our schedule, our problems, and our worries rule us once again—we should ask ourselves: What is the value of time if we don't understand the value of each breath? If now is not important to me, how can yesterday be important? If now is not important to me, how can tomorrow be important?

No matter what we plan, no matter what we do, no matter what happens, we can only live in this place called "now." That's where we are. Whether we are six months old or have made it to 100, on this journey we are all living in this moment. Many of us believe it's important to live in the here and now, but do we *know* the truth of this? Do we deeply appreciate now? Do we give gratitude for now?

There's a way of thinking about time that's quite different from the linear structure we are used to. It can be a little tough to grasp at first, but I'll try to describe it for you. Let's start with normal time. The convention is to divide our time up into smaller and smaller fractions: years, months, weeks, days, hours, seconds. Businesses are driven by time. More and more employees are monitored closely according to exactly how much they do in the time they're at work, sometimes down to the second. And if you've ever had a legal matter to resolve, you might have experienced the financial discomfort produced by a lawyer's timesheet!

There are sound reasons for dividing up our moments in this way. It helps to have a shared sense of time when you're arranging to meet friends for dinner or catching a plane or seeing a concert. But there are different perspectives on how we should think about time in a broader sense. Science, religion, and philosophy fizz with debate about what time is and how we might understand it. Empirically, it does seem as if—to use a spatial metaphor—time moves forward. I can say with confidence that if I broke my leg today, it wouldn't be whole by tomorrow, but it might be in six weeks' time.

However—and here is where it gets *really* interesting—we have another perspective on time available to us that we can use when we want to connect with something deeper. We can move in and out of this time frame as we wish when we know how to access it. You can think of it like this: in the external world, we see each moment as one unit in a passing set of moments, like a very long freight train going down the track. In the inner world, we can feel the moment as something absolute: a timeless today. Inner time is a beginning and an end in itself, like peace, energy, and light. It just *is*.

Imagine it this way: in each inner moment, the march of time is replaced by the dance of time. Just like me sitting beneath that magnolia tree, in the timeless today you are free to feel. No need to improve yourself or search for truth—you have found the infinite peace you're looking for. Here are some words from the celebrated English poet William Blake that resonate with this idea:

To see a World in a Grain of Sand
And a Heaven in a Wild Flower
Hold Infinity in the palm of your hand
And Eternity in an hour.

While we're thinking about infinity, it's important to know that there's no limit to how happy and contented we can be in the moment. People have died of too much sadness, but nobody has died of too much happiness. Let's keep filling our hearts with joy.

NETI NETI

I recognize that the concept of the infinite can be puzzling or frustrating. We try to use our minds to understand it, but it's tough to put a shape on something that can't fit easily into our imagination. My suggestion is: don't just respond to the idea of infinite time with your mind; let your heart try and feel it also.

Here's something that might help explain infinite time a little more. There's a Sanskrit phrase that captures the sense that an experience is beyond simple explanation or definition: *neti neti*. Literally, the term means "not this and not this" and is a fusion of two words, coming from *na iti, or* "not so." It's sometimes used when a person is trying to uncover the layers of themselves—"this is not me, neither is this, nor this"— until they get to the true "I." We're on the start of that same journey in this book: developing our capacity to leave normal time and the busy mind behind when we want to, to flow into the infinite so we experience the self in its purest form.

Often, when someone has had a profound experience, they can't capture it in words. In fact, they might not even know exactly what it was they encountered. Perhaps you know what this feels like. Sometimes, the essence of an experience is not present in the words we reach for to describe it. Language can be both useful and beautifully expressive, but it can't always take us into the heart of human experience.

A voice asks: "What was it you experienced? Was it this? Was it that?"

And you can only reply: "No, it wasn't quite that. Nor that."

"But what were you doing at that moment?"

"Nothing!"

"What were you thinking?"

"Nothing!"

"So what did you feel?"

"Everything!"

If experience can't be easily explained, people can assume it must be complicated in nature. But it's usually the attempt to explain it that's complicated, not the experience itself. Rather than presenting a clear and complete picture of what happened, sometimes we can only offer a shimmer of what went on. And sometimes an experience might be knowable but not expressible. Here are some lines on this from the poet Rumi:

> There is some kiss we want with our whole lives,
> the touch of Spirit on the body.
> Seawater begs the pearl to break its shell.
> And the lily, how passionately it needs some wild darling!
> At night, I open the window and ask the moon to come
> and press its face against mine.
> Breathe into me.

Close the language-door,
and open the love-window.
The moon won't use the door,
only the window.

When I walked from my family house in Dehra Dun into the garden, I wasn't thinking, "I'm now going to have an incredible experience." I started to enjoy each moment a little more, without understanding why, and then the wonder rose up inside me. It was blissfully simple, and I let it happen. My window was open.

There are times when people go into a garden and it's looking and smelling gorgeous, and they take their scissors and cut flowers for the house. I've done that, and it can be glorious to have a little of the color and perfume of the garden inside your home. But sometimes the opportunity is there for us to simply appreciate such beauty for what it is, without having to change it. Nature in a vase can be a lovely thing; encountering Nature *as it is* can be a fabulously pure and profound experience.

LETTING GO

To understand inner peace, we need to take away the bricks of intellectual concepts to reveal the natural shape and beauty of the self. You don't create peace; you *uncover* it inside you. It's a letting go of what isn't needed.

People talk about wanting to experience a revelation, but this is the revelation we're looking for: taking things away so we can reveal, understand, and experience our true self in its perfect simplicity. The French writer Antoine de Saint-Exupéry captured the elegance of simplicity when he said: "Perfection is not when there is no more to add, but no more to take away."

Think about your favorite shirt or dress for a moment. In your mind, go to your closet or drawers and lay it out on your bed. Get a really sharp mental picture of it. When you wear that shirt or dress, it will, after a while, get dirty. You're working or playing, traveling, running around, eating spaghetti—it's eventually going to get messy. So then you wash it. What is the process of cleaning? Very simple: you remove the dirt. You don't bring cleanliness from somewhere out there and put it inside the shirt. You take away what's not required and leave what's wanted: the clean item of clothing. It's the same with finding the peace within you. You do not add peace to your inner self; you let everything else fall away. Self-knowledge is about allowing your true self to shine in the present moment.

This reminds me of the apocryphal story about Michelangelo and the secret of great sculpture. "How on earth did you manage to create this sublime depiction of David?" the sculptor is asked. "Well," he replies, "I just kept chipping away everything that didn't look like David."

Follow the path of self-knowledge and you begin to focus right in on *you*, setting aside everything else. Then *you* become the constant. It's easy for other people to become the constant in our life and for us to only rarely glimpse ourselves. That's what happens when the noise dominates our life. We need to let go of the noise.

Can you imagine a state of being that is truly free from all these distractions? On the outside you have your body, and of course that will change. But there is something inside you that will stay the same regardless of events, regardless of other people. That's the timeless you.

FROM ABSENCE TO PRESENCE

But *how* do we let go of what we don't need? How do we let go of the noise? I have a suggestion: don't focus on the negative feelings within you—instead, strengthen the positives.

Presence and absence run through the universe. We can recognize both, but when it comes to our own life, we must choose what we want to make most present and most powerful. In my experience, it's far better if we encourage presence rather than try to manipulate absence. If we lack courage, then fear comes to the fore. What's the best way to counter fear? To draw on our courage and make it present once again. If you are not in touch with your clarity, then confusion comes. You remove the confusion by bringing your clarity. How do you remove crime? You help people live conscious lives, starting with yourself. To end darkness, bring in light.

Do you remember at school when the teacher would

walk in and ask: "Is everybody here?" That always made me laugh. The people who weren't there couldn't say: "No, I'm not here!" We can only work with what is present. So, we cannot simply get rid of hatred. That would leave a vacuum, and in Nature vacuums get filled with *something*. Instead, we need to choose love. If love is absent, it creates a vacuum that is quickly filled with hate. Bring love to the fore, and hatred fades.

When you think of a hole in the ground, is that something that *is* or something that *isn't*? Is it a thing with its own shape or is it merely an absence of something else? Holes exist but only because something else is not there. You can't move a hole from one place to another, right? I share my philosophy on holes with you because it can help us understand this point about presence and absence within us.

What is sorrow? The absence of joy.

What is confusion? The absence of clarity.

What is darkness? The absence of light.

What is war? The absence of peace.

War is a hole, an emptiness, a negation. So, how do we stop war? We fill it with something. And the best thing to fill it with is peace. Where can we find peace? Right inside each one of us. And where can we find the hole of war? Right inside each one of us.

So, that's how we can take the first steps toward peace between people: fill the holes of hatred, sorrow, confusion, darkness, and war inside us with the love, joy, clarity, light, and peace that are inside us.

A SYMPHONY OF SIMPLICITY

I once went to a classical music concert in Vienna. The hall was very crowded and there was a tremendous hubbub of excited conversation. The musicians came on stage and started to tune up. Then the talking got louder and people who were arriving at the last minute came in to take their seats, and that meant other people were having to stand up and sit down again to let them pass. It was a mess. I really didn't like it, actually: I could feel how unsettled my mind was becoming. I might easily have gotten up and walked out, but the tickets were hard to come by!

Suddenly the tuning stopped, the conductor came out, everyone applauded and . . . silence. There was a moment of delightful, hushed tension as the conductor raised and held his baton in midair. And then the music began. It was very quiet at first, and you could hear every resonance of the strings, the moving of fingers. It became an incredible sensory experience.

Sometimes it's like that inside us. There's a concert happening in our hearts. For some, the tuning up and the chatter last for years. For others, the baton goes up and peace comes in, and then the music starts. The noise, the silence, and the music are all inside us.

On occasion, there might also be a rhythm that moves us to dance—a rhythm stronger than all the other rhythms of life going on around us. Through self-knowledge we experience our true time signature, and we move in time to it. This is how it feels to be truly focused. Everything else drops away. There is silence, then a beautiful symphony starts to play in our heart. You hear yourself.

DETACHMENT, AMBITION, AND CHOICE

Should we aspire to be completely detached from the world around us? It's a question I'm asked often. My take on this is simple: you can't be 100 percent detached. Anyone who claims to live entirely free of the push and pull of everyday distractions is probably deluded.

Some people are anxious that self-knowledge will lead to a dull, abstract existence—a retreat from reality. If we gain contentment, do we become like a vegetable (a potato, perhaps, or a turnip) that's rooted to the spot? With nothing interesting going on in our potato or turnip brain, and no aspirations? Not at all! In some of the stories I've read about the life of the Buddha, I can see that he gained enlightenment and *then* became seriously ambitious. He wanted to take the message of peace everywhere right after he had found contentment.

I want to be really clear about this: self-knowledge does not transform our external self into a perfect being who can glide through life, untouched by questions and problems. What it can do is give us the clarity needed to recognize we have a choice. We have no choice over when we're born and when we die. We have a say in everything else.

Living consciously involves being aware that you *always* have a choice—even in rough times—then choosing carefully. We live unconsciously when we are unaware that we can choose, or we choose not to choose. One person's unconsciousness can lead to another person's unconsciousness, and so the cycle of ignorance continues. And it has consequences. On the other hand, becoming conscious of our choices can be tremendously empowering and fulfilling. I come back to this idea in chapter 5.

TRANSCENDING OUR WORRIES

It's tempting to think that if we get rid of all our worries, we will have peace. I can only speak from my own experience, which says this: If I stop thinking about food, will my hunger go away? No. And if somebody says to me, "Stop thinking about food!" will my hunger go away then? No. While you are alive you will probably go through times when you are worried about something—sometimes a little, sometimes a lot. That's when it pays to choose to move from your unsettled mind toward your peaceful heart, if you can.

I know people who have gone to the ends of the Earth in search of that one spot capable of giving them the worry-free mind they crave. What happens? They finally arrive and at last they settle into a chair. Then they close their eyes and think: "I'm here at last! Now I can really experience peace." All is quiet for a moment. Or two. And then they start to hear the crickets chirping. Or the wind rustling in the trees. Or waves lapping on the shore. Or a lonely bird singing somewhere far off in the woods. And then thoughts from home start to refill their mind, like luggage that was held up at the airport but has now been delivered.

Thus each man and woman constantly flees oneself—but to what end, if they do not escape oneself? When we are unsettled within ourselves, natural wonders can sound like a cacophony; when we are at home within ourselves, almost anything can become music. Unless we find the answer to the noise of worry, it will always travel with us. Our greatest defense is a capability we carry everywhere: knowing we can always choose to take the path of self-knowledge toward inner peace.

The poet Kabir said: "If you have to be worried, then worry about truth. If you have to be worried, worry about joy. If you have to be worried, worry about the good in your life." That's making worry absent by choosing to make positive qualities present.

LISTEN TO YOUR HEART

For me, the process of self-knowledge—from mindfulness to heartfulness and then peacefulness—is rather like the process of getting a rocket into space. Mindfulness is about calming the mind and focusing the attention: getting the rocket to the launch pad. We leave behind everything that's not needed for the flight and we focus our attention, so we're ready to go. Heartfulness is about fully connecting inside, so we can generate a powerful feeling of completeness that starts to lift us off the ground. And peacefulness is what we experience in our heart when we're going up, up, up—pulling away from gravity. And then the booster tanks drop away and we're flying into the vastness of our inner universe, beyond the dimensions of normal time and space.

My heart is the place inside me where I am deeply happy, not because of anything but happiness itself. There are oceans inside my heart which I sail, not to go anywhere but because it's such an incredible voyage. The heart is where we develop the courage to seek clarity in the midst of confusion, and where we can enjoy clarity for itself. I am in heaven when my heart is content, when it sings with gratitude for its existence. That's when I really feel alive. That's what I encountered on that magical morning in Dehra Dun.

We have to make sure we really do connect with our heart, and not our head's version of what our heart might want. That busy mind of ours is always ready to intrude and interpret everything its own way. Our mind finds it so very difficult to stop scanning the outside world for what's next. If it's an idea of the heart you have, well that's just more noise. Our heart is not there to be led or told what to feel; our heart simply expresses what it feels.

It's from being in peace that our priorities can be recognized most clearly, that our attention can be best directed. It's from experiencing the peace in our heart that we can best know ourselves. And this seems like a good moment to turn our attention to the difference between believing and knowing.

CHAPTER 4

Learn the Difference Between Knowing and Believing

How we think has a powerful impact on how we live. By marshaling our brainpower we can understand both the challenges and opportunities that face us, and doing so helps us make better decisions. At the same time, humankind's collective intelligence is enabling us to shape the world to our mutual advantage. The rise in average living standards is just one example that shows the impact of big thinking on our lives.

So, we should celebrate the power of the brain—but it's also smart to see thinking's limitations. We interact with the world in many different ways, yet in most modern societies it's thinking that dominates how people lead their lives. Many people try to house everything they encounter within the framework of what they *believe*, but that seems a rigid way to respond to the richness and flow of existence, to the wonderfully complex and messy busyness of life.

I feel there is a more fulfilling way to relate to the world inside and outside us. For me, the sweet spot of human experience is when we are intellectually alive to what's new but fully centered in our self. That way, our mind is open to change while our heart keeps us grounded in who we are. Through self-knowledge we can start to sharpen our focus on what's happening inside us: not ignoring the world, just adding to believing with also *knowing*—knowing what really matters. At a time when thinking is often valued above all else, this conscious balancing of our self is radical.

FINDING THE LIMITS OF THOUGHT

What's the problem with letting our mind dominate our experience of life? Well, because thoughts and beliefs often struggle to explain and express important aspects of who we are.

Imagine this scenario: you sit down with the person you care for most in the world and ask them: "Do you love me?" And they reply: "I think so." They *think* they love you? Or what if they said: "I believe so." They *believe* they love you? They might as well have answered: "No way!" You *know* whether you love someone or not.

Here's another simple question that can reveal the limits of thinking: Who are you? People often struggle to answer this question because it requires them to go beyond belief into feeling. We cannot answer it in a meaningful way by giving our name, age, gender, job, marital status, and favorite color. We cannot answer it in a meaningful way through logic or theory. It's about having a connection with yourself that is so deep and clear, you don't need to respond through words— you just *know*.

Swami Vivekanand, the Indian Hindu monk who was an international spokesman for the philosophy Vedanta, once said: "To believe blindly is to degenerate the human soul. Be an atheist if you want, but do not believe in anything unquestioningly." Believing is popular partly because somebody else has done our homework for us. It's not like we don't understand the consequences of blindly believing; it's just that it seems so much easier than knowing. But in reality, knowing is really not that hard: it's about knowing *your* self, not knowing something or somebody else.

AN INNER UNIVERSE

When Socrates said, *"Know* thyself!" it was an invitation to experience the innermost universe inside you. And what do you encounter when you get to that place of knowing within? Not a list of your beliefs. Not the revelation of your character traits, personality types, or psychological indicators. Not a theory of who you are. What you encounter is a feeling of infinite peace and a heartfelt appreciation of your presence in the moment. This is the complete connection of you with the universal power. And it's that rarest of experiences in a world of noise and busyness: the joy of just being.

The reasoning of the mind expresses itself through a line of questions. Who? What? Where? When? How? Why? And so on. These can be incredibly helpful in our daily lives, but they won't take us all the way to the infinite. To experience what *is*, in the deepest sense, we have to get away from the mind's framework. It's when we let the questions drift away that we start to *know*.

This is why, in India, self-knowledge is called Raj Yoga. *"Yoga"* doesn't mean "bend yourself into all sorts of positions"; it means "union." *Raj* means "king." So, *Raj Yoga* is the King Yoga that puts you in union with the divine, the greatest of all unions. And the divine isn't something mysterious hidden up a mountain—it's the peace in your heart.

My heart talks to me in the same direct way that my body expresses itself. When your body gets hungry, it tells you. When your body gets sleepy, it tells you. When your body is in pain, it tells you. No "please" is offered or expected. There are no niceties or manners. "You're hungry: you better eat something," it says. Self-knowledge enables you to hear your inner self clearly, so when your heart is fulfilled, you *know*. When your heart is full of joy, you *know*. When your heart is full of love, you *know*. The language of inner peace is clear, strong, and immediate. It has a simple poetry to it that is a delight to hear.

FINDING OUR WAY

What is the first rule of navigation for pilots? Know where you are! A map is useless if you don't know your location, however accurate and detailed it may be. Believing without knowing the self is like having a map but not understanding where you are on it. If you don't know where you are, how are you going to get where you want to go?

Pilots can experience something called "loss of orientation," and when that happens, they don't *know* their attitude, altitude, or airspeed. They are not where they think they are. In fact, they're lost and confused. We can experience something a little similar in our daily lives. Without knowing the self, we may have many ideas and plans but little sense of what really matters. Without knowing the self, we may have endless questions that take us further and further from a satisfying answer. Without knowing the self, we may feel a constant need to search for peace without ever experiencing the peace already within.

I'm inviting you to know where you are in this moment by *also* looking within and appreciating your existence in the here and now. In this way, self-knowledge is all about you knowing your *present position*. What is the most important thing that we can ever know? That we are blessed with life and the opportunity is there for us—every single one of us—to feel fulfilled each day, each hour, each minute. When you're connected to the peace inside, you get to truly enjoy the journey of life, experiencing joy and contentment right *now* rather than waiting until you reach your imaginary destination tomorrow.

MEANING COMES FROM WITHIN

What's inside us is the starting point for all meaning. We may look out of the window and think: "Ah, isn't the world beautiful!" without realizing that beauty starts within us. If humankind became extinct, beauty would disappear with us because beauty comes from us. You are carrying an infinite universe of beauty around inside you, right now. Self-knowledge is the path that takes us to all those wonders that sit inside us, waiting for our attention.

Think about the sweetness of a mango. All the ingredients needed to produce that incredible flavor are in the fruit, but it only comes to life when we open up the mango and enjoy it. Without our desire for flavor and our thirst for the juice, the mango would just be an object with certain chemical properties. When we add our desire and thirst, eating the mango becomes a delicious experience. Ultimately, the gorgeous sweetness of life is inside you, there to be tasted.

You are very thirsty and someone offers you a choice of either a glass of cold water or a thirty-minute presentation on the qualities of a glass of cold water—which are you going to choose? Obvious! Rather than try to satisfy our thirst for self-knowledge by developing a theory of who we are, we can always choose to *experience* who we are.

Without experience, everything we think and believe is theory. We can become addicted to theories, hoping they will miraculously explain everything. And then we start to bend reality to fit our ideas. I'm reminded of a quip I heard from an economist: "The idea works very well in practice, but does it work in theory?"

Theory has many uses—critically important uses sometimes—but it has its limits. Imagine a man who has promised his partner that he will make a delicious meal to celebrate their anniversary.

"What have you made for dinner, darling?"

"Oh, I love you so much that I spent all afternoon thinking about what I wanted to make for you," he replies.

"Sounds good!"

"But I didn't actually make you anything."

"Oh."

This is rather like some philosophical debate. It can be interesting to assemble the best intellectual ingredients that go into *being human*, but how much more exciting if they're then transformed into experience. This isn't an argument against philosophical inquiry; I'm just noting that ideas and theories about who we are only get you so far. Life isn't theoretical.

WHAT IS KNOWABLE?

We can be distracted by theorizing about the self and miss the opportunity to *know* our self. What is knowable? We can know that we are alive, that these moments we are moving through are real, that we can enjoy each moment to the full, that inner peace brings the ocean-deep sense of fulfillment that we seek, that when we are at peace, both the inner and outer worlds can shine ever more brightly for us, in all their glory. Knowledge is not an explanation; it's about experiencing the divine inside you.

The simple truth of this is right in front of us, but over-thinking can distract us from simple truths. As the ancient Greek dramatist Euripides put it, "Cleverness is not wisdom." Sometimes it seems as if people are reading a two-thousand-page guide to a one-page book, and the more they read the less they understand.

There's an old story about this that I like. The smartest people in the region came together to figure out which is more important: the Sun or the Moon. They deliberated and deliberated and deliberated, going back and forth. Finally, they came to a conclusion: the Moon is more important. And why is the Moon more important? "Look," they said, "in the daytime, when there is plenty of light, the Sun shines. But at night, when it's dark, the Moon shines. So it's clearly much more important."

First time I heard that story, I laughed and thought, "That's ridiculous." And then it occurred to me: actually, this is how we think sometimes. We can forget to appreciate the essentials in our life—the vital elements right in front of our nose. When we recognize this, and start to appreciate what's truly important, it's as if a light shines on us, illuminating the incredible gift we've been given.

FINDING THE CLEAR PATH

I was once traveling by car in the London rush hour when, up ahead, I saw someone walking down the street in a very particular way. They were moving at a normal pace, but, even from some distance, I could tell their body language was a little different from those around them. As I got closer, it became obvious that the person—a man on his own—couldn't see, and he was using his stick to feel his way.

I had observed plenty of visually impaired people walking with a stick before, so that wasn't what caught my eye. It was that this man showed no outward concern about the wall to the right of him, or the road to the left, or the other potential obstacles all around. He was using the stick to map out just enough of a clear area for him to keep moving safely. The man had a purposeful movement that suggested he wasn't getting mentally distracted by the passing traffic, the man and woman outside a shop talking, the music coming from the car parked up ahead, the big barking dog on the other side of the road, and so on. He knew where he was, and he was asking one clear question all the time: Do I have a free pathway in front of me so I can continue?

I thought how effective his approach was compared to the way we can end up mentally moving through our lives. Sometimes we imagine potential obstacles and problems everywhere. We see dangers where they don't exist and miss the ones that are there. We allow our attention to be taken by what moves around us rather than where we are now and where we want to go next. When we see the mountain, it can overwhelm us, but the pathway goes around the mountain. We get stuck thinking about all the obstacles before us and stop seeing the simplicity of the clear way ahead.

What does the visually impaired person do when they reach an obstacle? They feel their way to a clear path around it. What do we do when we encounter an obstacle in our minds? Often we just keep walking into it, hoping it will somehow move of its own accord.

I want to emphasize this point: in my experience, having self-knowledge doesn't magically clear our path of obstacles. What it can do is help us see the clear path. We can then choose what we do in response. If we focus on what's important to us, and we keep feeling for the clear path, we can keep moving forward.

I know that, at times, our life can seem dominated by obstacles, and that feeling may become overwhelming. I also know that people often see big obstacles to gaining self-knowledge, to experiencing joy, to seeing peace thrive in their heart, to having clarity and to making good choices. But these are just beliefs, and I *know* there really is a clear path for us when we choose to connect with the peace inside and start from there.

A CONVERSATION BETWEEN HEAD AND HEART

In putting more emphasis on feelings, is there a danger that our emotional responses to the world go unquestioned? Perhaps there is. We know that our feelings don't always match reality. We can all be unhelpfully irrational at times. Our emotions can also be heavily shaped by our mind. If we don't know our self, we can be fooled by anything, including our emotions, but through self-knowledge we're trying to connect with a deeper set of feelings.

What I've found helpful is listening carefully to both my thoughts and my deepest feelings, so they are in balance. If they seem to disagree with each other, it's probably a good time to invite the heart and mind to sit around a table and talk. And if we're going to do that, we might also invite along another part of us to that conversation: our instinct or intuition—the sum of all our experiences.

Our mind is often the loudest contributor to our internal conversation—we can always hear the chorus of who, what, where, when, how, and why—so it can be helpful to nurture the heart's voice. While the mind may be busy talking to us about expectations, plans, aspirations, and anxieties, the heart will simply say one thing many different ways: "Be fulfilled." And that's why, for me, the most meaningful answer to the question "Who are you?" is to be found in the heart.

While our mind is always trying to create meaning, our heart beautifully overflows with meaning. Take that earlier example of love: no explanation is ever required for it. Our mind can try to give us reasons, but we either feel it in our heart or we don't. We cannot really explain why we feel it: love just *is*. How wonderful is that?

It's the same with peace: it just *is*, in our heart. The thirst for peace is in us and the source of peace is in us. This is why it's always fascinating talking to someone about peace for the first time, because we must both start in our minds—understanding each other through words first—and then try to glimpse the formless beauty of inner peace. Ultimately, peace makes sense as a feeling. Through this book, I'm conveying what I feel peace can be for us, in our lives, but only you can experience it and understand it for yourself.

THE IMPORTANCE OF QUESTIONING EVERYTHING

Our mind is full of what it has been given over the years—of what we have chosen to accept and believe. We carry our beliefs around with us, and sometimes they can seem like heavy baggage, weighing us down. Imagine for a moment letting go of your bags full of beliefs. Imagine how light that would make you feel, how open to new ideas and experiences.

It's worth considering how we learn what we believe and what we know. For example, rote learning—memorizing through repetition—is one way we gather information from our parents. We use it in adult life too. The first time I visited Japan, I really wanted to learn how to say "thank you," so I asked some friends.

"Arigatou gozaimasu," they replied.

"What?" I said.

"Arigatou gozaimasu!"

"Whaat!?" It sounded so complex to my ear.

"Arigatou gozaimasu!"

"Hmmm . . ."

Slowly they helped me unpack it, understand it, and practice saying the words until the phrase meant something to me, then I could share it in conversation. And they did the same with some other useful phrases. It was about making the words my own.

So, rote learning can be useful, but we have to be careful not to cling to everything we are told. Growing up, our parents and teachers shared their understanding of the world with us. Part of becoming independent is being prepared to reconsider what you've been taught. The assumptions we make and the questions we ask of life: Are they *our* assumptions and questions? Much of the noise between our ears really belongs to someone else, but we always have the option to turn down the volume of their voice so we can hear ourselves.

Your parents probably told you things with good intent, but they weren't necessarily right. Generation after generation after generation, wrong ideas get handed down like broken heirlooms, and we carry these inherited ideas around with us in that heavy bag. We can probably all think of "truths" our parents and teachers lived by that now seem plain wrong. We just need to keep questioning what we have learned so we keep seeing the world clearly—not through other people's eyes, but through our own.

One day, in a science class at school, the teacher said: "Go to page 132 of your physics book." So we went to the page, and after a few minutes of reading the text, the teacher pointed out that it wrongly defined the atom as being indivisible. "Cross that out!" he shouted. And that made me wonder: everyone who took this class the year before had used this book, and in their minds the atom might still be indivisible! Now I don't know what difference believing that had made for them, but the whole episode taught me that it's good not to be fixed on any theory.

Over the years, I've seen that inherited ideas can be a block to us learning something new, whereas what we've learned through experience encourages us to open up to a world of possibilities. Perhaps we gain more confidence from experience than from ideas?

We have this wonderful opportunity to live life consciously and not unthinkingly follow the beliefs of our parents and teachers (which is really just intellectual reincarnation). And that's why I invite you to be aware of how my words resonate with you. Don't simply believe them; test them, not against your theories but your experience.

JUST BE QUIET

When someone starts to question our beliefs, it can provoke fear in us. Belief and fear get wrapped around each other like two thorn bushes growing side by side. It's really hard to pull them apart. If you live with fear, it's tempting to find refuge in beliefs, but beliefs can sometimes lead to yet more fears.

I find it helpful to approach learning by remembering the mind–heart balance I mentioned earlier: my mind should be open to constant change, but my heart is unchangeable. That gives me strength at my core, but also a willingness to hear other points of view. Here's an old story that comes to mind about being open to new ideas and learning from others.

Once, a young man was seeking to become wise, so he started to look for a wise man. He searched and searched until he found someone who seemed to fit the description. He approached this wise man and said: "Could you please give me wisdom?"

At first the wise man seemed reluctant. "Are you really ready to receive wisdom?" he asked.

"Absolutely," said the man, "I have been searching for years. I have traveled far and wide, and I am ready."

The wise man thought for a moment and said: "OK, I will teach you, but first I have to water my crops. Please come with me to the well and wait while I draw water. Also, I have one condition: whatever happens, just be quiet and say nothing. After I've finished watering my plants, I will give you wisdom."

The student thought to himself: "This is very good, all I have to do is be quiet, watch him water his plants, and then he will give me wisdom!"

They went to the well, and the wise man threw his bucket down the hole. After a minute or so he pulled the bucket back up and it was full of holes, so it leaked water everywhere until it was soon empty. Immediately, the wise man picked up the empty bucket and threw it down the well again.

The student started thinking: "Hmm, that's odd. Is he really so wise? Doesn't he know that his bucket is full of holes?

How is he going to water the plants, because every time he brings the water up the bucket's empty?" But then he thought: "OK, all I have to do is be quiet and he will give me wisdom."

The wise man pulled up the bucket. Once again, water poured from the holes and it quickly emptied. The student could feel his doubts rising inside him, but he said to himself: "Just be quiet and you will get wisdom."

A third time, the bucket came up and was pouring water from its holes. It was empty in no time, yet the wise man just threw it back down the well. The student was really beginning to doubt now. "Why does he not see that the bucket is leaking and full of holes? Can this man really be a teacher?"

For a fourth time, the bucket reappeared from the well with water spilling from the holes, and the wise man once again threw it back down the well. The student was thinking: "What is wrong with this man? Can he really teach *me* anything?"

For a fifth time, the wise man pulled up the bucket and it was leaking water all over the side of the well and creating a huge pool of water on the ground. This time the student couldn't hold back any longer. He said to the wise man: "Excuse me; don't you know that your bucket is full of holes and it cannot hold anything?"

The wise man let the bucket drop, smiled, and came to sit by the student. "It is true, the bucket is full of holes and cannot hold water. And you've shown that your bucket has many holes and cannot hold anything. Your mind is full of beliefs, just as this bucket is full of holes."

As with lots of the old stories, the conclusion here is simple—

if your mind is already full of beliefs, it will be difficult for you to learn anything else from others—but the wisdom flows outward, like the ripples from a stone thrown into a pond. Or a well.

Once, a skeptic came to see my father speak. He was planning to heckle from the back and was waiting to find exactly the right moment to object to something—a message, a story, whatever. That forced him to listen very carefully to what my father was saying. Every word. He never did heckle. In fact, by the end of the session, he was pretty much ready to ask my father for Knowledge. He came with a set of preconceptions and a plan, but he opened up enough to let his heart listen, as well as his head.

NEEDING TO KNOW

People sometimes say to me: "Oh come on, get real—all this talk about inner peace is a fantasy!" In fact, there are many people who doubt that peace is possible. Some reach this conclusion after careful consideration, and I respect that. Others simply write off peace in a heartbeat. If you don't have self-knowledge in your life, big principles like "peace is possible" can be threatening. Some people are afraid to let any kind of doubt enter their house of strong beliefs.

Doubts can drive us crazy. If you doubt that the person you love is true to you, the fear involved is not going to be talked away by theory. We need to *know*.

Let me dramatize this for you. (It's helpful to know that

Akbar was a sixteenth-century Indian ruler and Birbal was his advisor.)

One day the wife of Akbar, the Emperor, came up to him and said: "You favor your adviser Birbal above my brother. He's your relative, you should be putting him first. Birbal is a nobody!"

Akbar replied: "Yes, I do favor Birbal. He's witty and smart."

His wife said: "So is my brother and I want him appointed."

Akbar said: "Well, how is this going to happen?"

And she said: "Very simple: you take a walk in the garden. Call Birbal. Tell him to come and fetch me. I will not come and then you can fire him for his failure."

Later, Akbar was walking in the gardens and he said: "Call Birbal." Quickly, Birbal came.

"Yes, your Majesty? What can I do for you?"

"Go fetch my wife. I would like her to be here while I'm taking my walks."

Birbal looked at Akbar and said: "Your Majesty, you have so many servants, why have I been given this honor?"

The Emperor had a smirk on his face. "No reason," he said, "I just choose you."

Birbal realized there was a problem. So he figured out what was going on: the Emperor's wife must have put him up to it. And he quickly deduced that the wife had no intention of coming.

On the way to visit the Empress, he stopped one of the guards and said: "I'm going to talk to her Highness. While I'm in the middle of speaking, come in and start whispering in my ear. I want you to say some words loud enough that she hears them. The words are: 'And she is *very* beautiful.'"

Birbal went and spoke to the Empress.

"Highness, the Emperor wishes for you to join him in the garden . . ." and so on, but he was getting nowhere with her. After a while the guard came in, started whispering in his ear and—as instructed—said: "And she is *very* beautiful." Then he left.

Birbal turned to the Empress: "Ah, your Highness, you don't need to come now, but I think I'm needed there." And he went out.

Two minutes later the Empress was by the Emperor's side in the garden. He turned to her and said: "You see, I told you Birbal is very smart. How did you do it, Birbal?"

And Birbal said: "Majesty, all I had to do was plant a little seed of doubt, and she had to know."

ON TEACHING

Many times my father would say to my brothers and me: "I never understood how, but my Master answered all the questions I hadn't even asked." One of the things we learned from my father was how to listen and then contemplate what we'd been taught. Often, the questions became clear after I had truly heard the answers.

I'm so thankful for what my father gave me, especially that gift of being able to go inside myself and feel fulfilled. The relationship of father and son ended a long time ago, when he passed away, but the gift that he gave me keeps bearing fruit. My ambition is to share the seeds of that fruit with as many people as I can.

It wasn't always easy being thought of as a teacher when I was young. I remember looking out at big rooms and seeing doctors, lawyers, and many other mature and educated people sitting patiently, waiting for me to speak. There I am, nine or ten years old; they in their thirties, forties, fifties—and they're waiting to ask *me* questions. And I'm going to give them answers.

When I spoke, people would often ask me: "But how do you *know* this?" And my answer was always: "Because I have *experienced* this." And then people might say: "Can you show me?" And I would answer: "Yes, but first you need to feel your thirst for peace." That's because preparing for self-knowledge starts with you acknowledging your desire to *know yourself.*

There's no point setting out on this journey if you want to confirm your existing beliefs; it's about feeling the need to experience who you *really* are. It's like when you give a wrapped gift to a child. They start to ask: "What is it? Is it *this*? Is it *that*? I think I know what it is!" They're trying to match the shape of the gift to what they want it to be. But the only way they can know what's inside is to remove the layers of wrapping paper. It's the same with the self.

In India, when my speaking tours finished, I used to go back to school and then *I* became the student again. Sometimes that was as difficult for the teacher to adjust to as it was for me. In one moment I was being listened to with great attention; the next day teachers were shouting: "You're late!" (And I probably *was* late.)

So, I asked myself, who am I? My answer started with this simple thought: "My life is ever-changing, but through self-knowledge I'm always going to be connected to my self." With great clarity I saw that nothing is going to last forever, so I needn't get concerned about moving between different roles in my life. I thought: "I'm not going to be a student forever, but when I'm at school, I can be *that* version of me." And: "I'm not going to be a child all my life, but while I am, I can be that son." And: "I'm not necessarily going to be a speaker about wisdom in India all of my life, but while I'm here, I can be that."

Understanding that nothing in life is fixed was liberating. It enabled me to be more flexible in my outlook, and that made some of my difficult teachers much easier to bear.

SUSPENDING BELIEF

"Wisdom begins with wonder," said Socrates, once again encapsulating a profound truth in a few words. The same thought resonates in the English poet Coleridge's desire for readers to allow their imagination a "willing suspension of disbelief for the moment, which constitutes poetic faith."

Born in 1772, Samuel Taylor Coleridge wanted people to free themselves from their logical mind when reading, so they could experience something *other*—something beyond what they already thought. In this spirit, Coleridge set about a project called the *Lyrical Ballads*, collaborating with his fellow poet William Wordsworth to create a collection of highly imaginative poems. Coleridge described Wordsworth's goal as one of

> awakening the mind's attention from the lethargy of custom, and directing it to the loveliness and the wonders of the world before us; an inexhaustible treasure, but for which in consequence of the film of familiarity and selfish solicitude we have eyes, yet see not, ears that hear not, and hearts that neither feel nor understand.

In a similar spirit, what we're aiming for here is *a willing suspension of belief.* Yes, we'll always need smart thinking and sound ideas to inform how we understand the world. Science produces enormous benefits for us all. But when it comes to self-knowledge, we must quiet our thinking and listen to the deepest voice within. We need to have eyes that truly see, ears that truly hear, and hearts that truly feel and understand—that truly *know.*

Along with developing our mind, where is the harm in a willing suspension of belief that awakens our attention from the lethargy of rote living, and directs it to the wonders of the world before us—and within us?

CHAPTER 5

Start with You

A young man was walking down the road when he saw a much older man, bent over by the weight of the huge bundle of wood that he was carrying on his back. The young man thought to himself: "This fellow has been around for a long time, while I'm just starting out—why don't I ask him for some wisdom?" So he went over and said: "Old man, please give me some advice on life." The man looked at him, took the heavy load from his shoulders, put it down, and stood up straight. Then he looked at him again, bent down, lifted the wood back onto his shoulders, stood up, and walked away.

What's the moral of this story? Perhaps it's that we should limit the burdens we carry. Or maybe it tells us that much of life is simply about getting on with what's necessary, and we should avoid giving time to distractions. Or that sometimes we can say more by showing rather than telling. But what I *always* take away from this tale is a reminder that life demands we stand on our own two feet. We may need help from others now and then, but ultimately we must take responsibility for ourselves. That's what this chapter is about.

SAILING OUR OWN SHIP

Let's back up a little. When we were born, we were at the center of our world. None of life's complexities and confusions had affected us yet, and we were able to express the pure energy of being alive and having needs. Think of the natural way a baby laughs or cries. Think of a child's wide smile when they're enjoying themselves. Why do we ever let these feelings go? As adults, we can become like actors performing for other people, trying to keep everyone else happy. But where is *our* joy? Where is *our* love? Where is *our* peace? They are always deep within us, but sometimes we forget they are there.

When this disconnection to our self happens, we may look to the outside world for answers. Other people can help us—through anything from kind listening to expert guidance—but ultimately *we* have to find that connection back to who we really are. Ultimately, only I am responsible for my happiness, and only you are responsible for your happiness.

DO YOU APPROVE OF YOU?

Sometimes we wrongly believe that whatever our family, friends, and colleagues think about us is what we *are*. We can end up molding our opinions to fit with what they think—or what we *think* others think. We can become like those politicians who constantly consult opinion polls to check their approval ratings, and only say what they believe people want to hear. But other people's opinions and your own needs are two different things. The Roman Emperor and philosopher Marcus Aurelius put it like this:

> Every man's happiness depends from himself, and yet behold, thou dost make thy happiness to consist in the souls and conceits of other men.

It's tough to respect someone who doesn't respect oneself. In fact, we see the need for acceptance everywhere we look. People worry about what strangers think of their appearance. People worry about whether they've said something smart in meetings. People worry about whether they're likable. More important than all that: Do *you* approve of you? Do *you* like spending time with you? Do *you* understand and appreciate yourself? This is not about being self-centered; it's about being centered in your self.

DON'T TAKE OFFENSE, DON'T GIVE OFFENSE

At home, at work, at school, in public—we can feel we are constantly judged and then *we* return the favor by judging everything back. We judge people for being judgmental! So a negative atmosphere can build, like a weather system, and before you know it, there are storms.

Imagine two chemicals that are stable on their own but

explode when combined: now think of them as the desire you and another person have to judge each other. Mix the two chemicals together and you start the process of emotional combustion.

But there's another way. It's not always easy to do, but if we stop judging other people, and focus on how much we approve of ourselves, it transforms everything. When we feel centered in our self, it doesn't trouble us to hear other people's opinions, whatever they may be.

One mantra I find useful is "Don't take offense, don't give offense." Put another way, if you don't take on board a cargo of negative comments, you won't feel the need to dump them at the next port.

When we feel the temptation to focus on someone else's character, we can instead focus on ourselves. How am *I*? Do *I* understand myself? Am *I* being kind and loving to others? Am *I* feeling the peace within me? I say to myself: don't look for kindness from others until you've found the kindness in you. Don't look for love from others until you've found the love in you. Don't look for peace in others until you've found the peace in you.

The poet Rumi captured this beautifully:

Yesterday I was clever, so I wanted to change the world.
Today I am wise, so I am changing myself.

That same wisdom was reexpressed some 600 years later by the Russian writer Leo Tolstoy:

. . . in our world everybody thinks of changing humanity, and nobody thinks of changing himself.

To put all this another way—start with yourself.

IT'S NONE OF YOUR BUSINESS

I came across a wonderful saying that reminds us there's another way we can respond to criticism: "What other people think about you is none of your business." Yes! If someone you respect makes a sound point about you, fine—learn from it. Otherwise, just go your own way.

A husband and wife went on a long journey and started out walking alongside their horse. Some villagers saw them and said: "That couple are crazy: they have a horse but they're not riding it."

The man and woman overheard this and said to each other: "OK, let's ride the horse." So they both sat on it.

At the next village, some people came out of their houses to watch the strangers and they said: "How cruel those people are: they are both riding that poor horse."

Again, they both overheard these comments. The man thought to himself: "I must show sympathy to the horse and to my wife," so he invited her to sit while he walked, and she did.

At the next set of houses some more people came out, and they said: "See this girl; she hasn't any sympathy in her heart toward her husband."

So, to protect his wife from criticism, the man said: "Come down, I'll sit on the horse."

Of course, at the next place the villagers said: "Haven't you got any sympathy for your wife, not even one bit? You are riding and she is walking!"

So the man came down and said: "Wife, if we're going to believe these people, we will never reach our destination. Let's go as we were." And they continued their journey, walking alongside their horse.

WHO CARES?

In India, most families manage their spending very carefully—they have to—but when it comes to their daughter's or son's wedding, they will often splurge in the most remarkable way. People sometimes take out loans much greater than their annual income. They will borrow because they want to make a good impression. That happens all over the world, but Indians have it down to a fine art. And then they have to pay the bill.

Here's a tip that could save you many thousands: only invite people to your wedding who already love and respect you! This also works well for birthdays, anniversaries, and other big social events. But here's the real point: if you're looking to achieve perfection on the outside—in other people's eyes—you're probably going about things the wrong way. Other people's perceptions of you cannot be controlled. Their feelings shift and evolve. When we trust and appreciate ourselves, other opinions of us are just a passing thing—sometimes unfair, sometimes accurate, sometimes even pleasurable, but never of lasting importance. What endures is what I feel about me, and what you feel about you.

In many cases, those passing judgment are not *really* thinking about us—they're more likely to be thinking about what we think about them! Or maybe it's as American newspaper advice columnist Ann Landers once remarked: "At age 20, we worry about what others think of us. At age 40, we don't care what they think of us. At age 60, we discover they haven't been thinking of us at all."

Once, when I was speaking to inmates at a prison in Pune, India, a prisoner stood to ask me a question. "I am here for the wrong reasons," he said. "I mean, *I* shouldn't be here, but I'm going to be let out shortly and will be going back home. What are the people there going to think about me?"

I quickly realized how important this issue is for many inmates, because every single person turned to look at him. His question had struck a nerve. There were hundreds and hundreds of people in that room, so it was quite a moment. The place went silent, and then everyone turned back to look back at me, wondering what I was going to say.

I responded: "Do you really want to know?"

And he said he did.

"Well, I'm sorry to tell you this," I said, "but they haven't been thinking about you. They've got their own problems! You are thinking about what they are thinking about you, but most people are busy thinking about other things. You believe they're only sitting there and thinking about you? Well, you may be important, but not *that* important. People move on!"

The inmates seemed to find this perspective helpful, perhaps because we all know that when it comes to other people judging us, there are always "two schools of thought." It's almost absurd: in our head, we're imagining what's going on in their head, even though in our head we realize it isn't that important; and in their head they're probably thinking about something else! Round and round it goes. It can take time and effort, but the solution is to give your energy to what you *can* know: who *you* are, within your heart. Everything else is noise.

BUDDHA'S BOWL

For anyone who has ever felt discouraged by others, I would like you to hear these words very clearly: *you* have the power to decide what's right for *you*. I'm here to remind you of that power, to tell you it is alive and well inside you, to suggest that you try to connect closely with that strength inside you, and to invite you to stand up for yourself once more. To be discouraged is to have your courage hidden from you—but it's *your* courage, and the possibility is always there to find and feel the courage within.

One time, Buddha was walking with a disciple, and everybody in town was criticizing him, saying: "You're no good. You don't do this, you don't do that . . ."

The disciple said: "Buddha, doesn't it bother you that all these people are criticizing you?"

Buddha waited until they got back to his home, then he took his bowl and moved it toward the disciple.

He said: "Whose bowl is it?"

And the disciple said: "It's your bowl."

So he moved it a little closer to the disciple.

"Whose bowl is it?"

"It's still your bowl."

He kept doing this, and the disciple kept saying: "It's your bowl; it's your bowl."

Then Buddha took the bowl and put it in the disciple's lap, and said: "Now whose bowl is it?"

The disciple said: "It's still your bowl."

"Exactly!" said Buddha. "If you don't accept this bowl, it's not yours. If I don't accept criticism, it's not mine."

NO GRUMBLING

If we're not careful, one person's negativity can cast a cloud over everyone else. That's probably why Saint Benedict, the sixth-century founder of the Benedictine Holy Order, was so against grumbling (it comes up time and again in The Rule of Saint Benedict, Benedict's "rulebook" for life in a monastery). You can just imagine how irritating a grumbler would be if you were living in a monastery with them twenty-four hours a day.

This reminds me of a joke. A young man joins a monastery,

and on the first morning, they explain to him: "In this place we have one big rule: no speaking. But once a year we'll ask you how it's going, and you get to say two words."

So the first year goes by and they ask him: "How is it?"

He says: "Too cold."

Another year goes by.

"How is it?"

"Bed hard."

And then the next year ends.

"How is it?"

"Too quiet."

Finally, the head monk comes to see him and says: "You've been here three years and you have done nothing but complain, complain, and complain."

EVERYTHING YOU NEED IS WITHIN YOU

Sometimes we might look for approval and other distractions to fill an empty feeling in ourselves. But no one else can fill that emptiness for us. They would be pouring water into a cracked bowl. We must accept ourselves, and that means accepting the wonderful strengths and resources inside us. Ultimately, we don't need to worry about other people's judgment, because everything we need is within us.

This is so important that I want to say it again: everything we need is within us! Clarity, joy, serenity, love—these and many other positive feelings are all inside you, waiting to blossom. And so are all the negative qualities too, of course. Clarity is in you, but so is confusion. Joy is in you, but so is despair. Serenity is in you, but so is chaos. Love is in you, but so is hatred.

Your negative qualities tend to just show up, but you may have to work a little to find the good in you. Positive qualities spring from your inner peace, and that gives you a rock-solid and unchangeable foundation at the heart of your being. But you have to know where to look for this treasure. Which leads me to a story.

A man leaves his village and goes to town to earn some money. He does very well for himself and, after a few years away, decides it's time to go back to see his family. So he sets off on the long journey home, his suitcases and bags packed with gifts. Almost immediately, a thief spots him and thinks: "This chap has money. I don't care about the little gifts, I want his purse." He goes up to the man and makes conversation. He asks where he's going, and then says: "Well, I'm heading in exactly the same direction, so let's travel together."

That night they check into an inn. Over dinner, the man reveals that he's done very, very well in the city and he's now going home to build a big house and take care of his family. The thief is delighted to hear this. He makes an excuse about going to bed early, but he goes to the man's room instead. He looks through every one of his bags but he doesn't find his money. He looks in every drawer but doesn't find it there. And he turns his bedding inside out but doesn't find so much as a single coin.

Next night they check into another inn. "So, you definitely made lots of money," says the thief, "and you're bringing it all home to build a house and take care of the family, right?"

"Oh yes," says the man, "I made much more money than I expected, and I'm really delighted I can bring it all home and make something beautiful."

Once again, the thief sneaks off and inspects the man's room, looking in every place he can think of. Nothing.

The following night they arrive at another inn and again the man joins the thief for dinner. At the end of their meal the thief says: "So, you'll soon be home and investing that money." "That's right," says the man, "it's going to be great." And, with that, the thief says goodnight and goes to desperately search every inch of the man's room for his purse. Nothing.

Next morning, they're nearing the man's home village, and the thief can no longer contain himself. "I have to confess something," he says. "I am a thief, and when you told me you had all this money, I really wanted it. Every night I checked your entire room, even looking inside your boots and under your pillow. I found nothing. Did you really make any money?"

"Oh yes," says the man cheerily, pulling two bulging purses from his pockets, "I realized you were a thief straightaway. So each night, on the way to dinner, I would go into your room and hide my fortune under your pillow. I knew you would check under mine, but never under your own."

To find the priceless treasure of inner peace, look within. No bazaar sells it, no landowner controls it, no government regulates it, and nobody can steal it from you. You are rich with self-knowledge and all the treasure that will enable you to discover the peace inside you.

We become experts at sensing the outside world—seeing, feeling, tasting, smelling, hearing—but did you know we can also project our senses inward? What are the textures and shapes of your inner world? What pictures do you see when you try to look inside yourself? What is the taste of your needs and desires? What is the scent of your emotions? What is the secret sound of the self within you? Can you hear yourself clearly?

When I was a kid, we had these books where you could paint by numbers: 1 meant red, 2 yellow, 3 blue, and so on. They were fun. Then these new books appeared where the paint was already on the page; you just needed to put water on and the picture started to appear. It was a bit simplistic. One day I thought, why go through this whole process? So I took the whole book and dipped it in water, let it dry, opened it—and everything was painted. But it didn't mean anything: it was just a mess. So I started to draw and paint from scratch.

There are a lot of people in this world who live their lives hoping to be told where to paint. They're saying: "Give me squares I can paint in or wash with water, just don't ask me to create something myself." But we've been given the opportunity to express ourselves—to paint beautiful pictures with the strengths we have inside. Each new morning, we can choose to be the most fantastic version of ourselves. Ignore the numbers. Paint outside the boxes. Paint what's in your heart. Paint the most dazzling version of who you are.

ONES AND ZEROS

A long time ago I was speaking at an event in Santa Cruz, California, and we finished with a question-and-answer session. I remember that the room was full; people were standing outside, looking in through the windows and doors. At one point, a woman—a yoga teacher—raised her hand to indicate that she had a question for me, and the attention in the room focused on her.

"What do you think of yoga?" she asked.

I might have misinterpreted the situation, but I felt she was expecting me to say: "Oh, yoga is something we *all* must do," and then she'd get more clients or more kudos. Looking back on it, I can see that my answer must have sounded absurd to her. I replied:

"Oh, yoga? Yeah, it's like zero."

Zero.

She was so ticked off. That wasn't the answer she was looking for at all, so she left. After she had gone, I went on to explain what I meant to those who were still in the room:

"Think of it like this: you are one and yoga is zero. Put zero in front of one, what do you get? One stays one, zero stays zero. Put zero *after* one, and you get ten. Add another zero, and you get a hundred."

I thought it was a rather brilliant answer, but I was too slow to explain my genius to the yoga teacher!

There is a serious point here: what we put in front of us doesn't add to us. Job, money, beliefs, other people's needs, yoga: they shouldn't come *before* us. On the other hand, what-ever we put *after* us multiplies what we are. First and fore-most, we must establish the one, because without that there's nothing. Then we can begin putting lots of zeros after that one.

There are seven billion ones in this world. I am a one. You are a one. In your life, everything needs to start with your par-ticular one—*you*.

WHAT WILL YOU CHOOSE?

When we understand who we really are, it gives us a very pow-erful tool. That tool shapes our lives and the world around us. I'm talking about choice. Self-knowledge enables you to see that you get to choose between peace and conflict, between love and hate, between joy and grumbling. Not choosing is also a choice, by the way. If you just choose to float on the river of life, you can't complain when it takes you somewhere you don't like.

We need to be conscious of what is happening in our life. When we're in a car or on a bicycle heading home, how do we know we're going in the right direction and not lost? Because everything we see is confirming where we are and where we're heading. In life, what are the clues along the way? Are we seeing them clearly? Am I conscious of where I am today and what I want to experience in this world?

Is it possible to be conscious all the time? No, because liv-ing unconsciously almost comes naturally to us: we're really good at it. But what if we choose to work at being conscious? Well, it can have a profound effect on us and on others. But we must always start with our self. You are the center of your universe, but you need to choose to understand and fully experience this—to *know* this.

What we choose in our lives will make all the difference for us and touch on the lives of those around us. Many people feel they have no choice, but we always do. *Always.* You may be in a terrible situation and feel that you have very little freedom, security, or opportunity—and those situations do happen to people, and they are frightening—yet even then, you can choose to connect with the peace inside you. But only *we* can make the choice; others cannot do it for us.

Moving through life can be rather like driving a car. Driving is all about making choices—where you steer, which gear you're in, how fast you go, where you stop, what you play on the radio. When you're in the driver's seat of your life, you are in charge and your decisions have consequences. Stop making good choices—and you can get lost, run out of gas, stall, or even crash! Make good choices—and you can go wherever you want and enjoy the ride.

Let's take this analogy a little further. When you're driving, if you look in the rearview mirror all the time, you miss what's coming up ahead. If you keep imagining what's around the next corner, you can miss what's going on right in front of you. It's much more satisfying to be in the moment: to see the road ahead clearly, to respond by making good choices, and to appreciate every mile of your journey. Are *you* in the driver's seat of your life?

GETTING STARTED

We start with ourselves when we choose to accept the gift of life given to us in each moment and understand that the gift is for *us*—to do with as we choose. We start with ourselves when we choose to listen to our heart, above the noise of other people's opinions, needs, and wants. We start with ourselves when we recognize that we have a world of peace and strength within, that the un-stealable treasures of the self are there for us whenever we choose to turn inside. We start with ourselves when we feel our thirst to know who we are.

Here are some lines from me on listening to my heart and the wonder of first encountering our self:

In darkness, you said learn to look
I was confused at first
But now I see.

Without a cup, you said learn to taste
I was thirsty at first
But now I have drunk.

Without moving, you said learn to touch
I was numb at first
But now I feel.

In silence, you said learn to listen
I was deaf at first
But now I hear.

We've covered a lot of ground in this chapter, so I'm going to leave you with a reminder of three simple ways we can all connect with ourselves:

- Know that everything we need is within us—sense the incredible array of resources you have inside.
- We have huge potential, but we must express it in how we live—there is no one else like you, so become the greatest version of who *you* can be.
- Remember, we always have a choice—whatever situation you're in, you have more than one option.

P.S. WHO IS THE IDIOT?

I can't resist adding this story to the end of the chapter. It's my version of a classic Akbar and Birbal tale. This one is about how we can waste time judging other people while not looking clearly at ourselves.

There was an Emperor in India, Akbar, and he called up his favorite minister, Birbal, because he needed help.

"Birbal, go find me five idiots."

"Yes Majesty," replied Birbal, and he left the room. As he was walking out, he was also thinking: "I said 'yes' to his request, but how am I going to find five idiots? Why did I agree to this? This is not going to be easy!"

Birbal was the smartest man in the court, but he was worried that he might not have a solution to this problem. So he put aside all of his other duties and went out into the street in search of idiots. He was wondering how he might approach this task when he saw a man lying on the ground, moving his legs around frantically while holding his hands wide apart.

"What are you doing?" asked Birbal.

"Well, my wife is redecorating our house, and she measured a window for curtain material, and she told me to go to the market and buy exactly this much curtain," he said, nodding toward the distance between his hands. "Then I fell, and I've been struggling here on the ground because I can't use my hands to get back up."

"Well, I think I found the first idiot," thought Birbal.

An hour or so later, he saw a man riding a donkey while balancing a huge basket on his head.

"What are you doing?" asked Birbal.

"Ah! I love my donkey: I wouldn't want to put this heavy load on him, so I'm carrying it on my head instead."

Birbal was delighted. Another idiot found.

It started to get dark, so Birbal went to stand by a street lamp, and there he saw a man on his hands and knees, looking for something on the ground.

"What are you doing?" asked Birbal.

"This afternoon I was with my friends in the jungle, about a mile from here," said the man. "We were having a picnic and I was wearing my ring, but the ring fell off."

"Well, shouldn't you be looking for the ring in the jungle?" said Birbal.

"Are you crazy?" said the man. "There is no light in the jungle at this hour, it's dark!"

Birbal rubbed his hands together in glee.

Next day Birbal took the three men to meet the Emperor.

"Lord, I found your idiots," he said, then explained what each one was doing when he encountered them.

"But Birbal, I asked you for five idiots," said the Emperor.

"Lord, the fourth idiot is me for wasting all of yesterday looking for idiots," said Birbal.

"And the fifth idiot?" asked the Emperor.

Birbal just smiled.

CHAPTER 6

Choose Gratitude

When I ask people, "What are you grateful for in your life?" they often reply with something like, "Oh, my family, my friends, my home, my job." That's all perfectly understandable—all of those things are of course wonderful blessings—but I sometimes feel that people are only really saying what they *think* they should be grateful for. I keep waiting for them to also acknowledge the most important gift any of us is given—life itself! Without that everything else is impossible, yet it can just slip our mind.

UNWRAPPING THE GIFT

I often hear people declare, "We need to live for today!" But how many of us really feel the truth of that in our hearts? How many times a day do we think: "I'm alive, thank you!" Is it the first thing that occurs to us in the morning, or does our mind instead carry us straight to the likes of "What time is it? What do I have to do today? Where's the toothpaste? I need coffee!" The noise. The noise. The noise. When we're tuned in to the noise, we stop hearing anything else—and we stop hearing ourselves.

The gift of life deserves to be unwrapped and treasured. (And by the way, there's definitely a "Use by" date on this gift, so start ripping off that wrapping paper!) Our hearts are filled with appreciation when we see, with absolute clarity, the opportunity we're given in each moment. And that's the gratitude I want to talk about here: the inner acknowledgment that every breath brings the blessing of life. And with that clarity comes an incredible feeling of fulfillment.

When my feeling of gratitude inside me expresses itself, it says: "I am alive and I truly *know* I am alive." Then I feel the life-force pulsing through me. Right now, the incredible energy that sustains the entire universe is sustaining me. My blood cells are transporting oxygen from my lungs to where it's needed. I have all these electrons, protons, and neutrons within me and around me. And each new breath is powering my existence here on this stunning planet, with all the possibilities that brings. A human being is a brilliantly constructed collection of complex parts and processes—an absolute living wonder—so what better gift can we give ourselves other than to appreciate our design and fully experience every moment?

In its purest and most potent form, my gratitude for this life is for the gift itself: not what it enables me to do, but just the experience of existing in this world, right now. This song of gratitude plays for me when I take the journey from the outside to the inside.

There are billions of us on the face of this Earth, and every person is unique in how they feel about what they've been given. Each one of us can sing a different song: a song about how I feel being alive, how I feel when I'm content, and how I feel when I'm joyful. Some don't know about the gift they've been given; others celebrate it often. Whoever you are, there is always that opportunity to feel gratitude for the greatest asset you will ever own.

FEELING GRATITUDE

Gratitude isn't something that we *think* into being; it's something we feel. We can feel fulfilled, but we can't think fulfilled. We can feel thankful, but we can't think thankful. It's not about thinking ourselves fortunate; it's about giving thanks for our life through how we feel.

Gratitude is not about good manners, either; it's me *choosing* to appreciate my existence in the way *I* feel. We are often cajoled into saying "thank you" for what we are given (children experience this all the time), but gratitude for life comes from within.

When is the right time to start feeling gratitude for our life? Now. There's no need to wait for a ceremony, or the alignment of planets, or a personal crisis. We just move our attention inside and appreciate what we are being given. In that perfect moment of gratitude, all distractions fade away. It's as if our journey has finally reached its destination, yet an exciting new journey is starting too. Gratitude is the perfect meeting point of past and present—a celebration of now.

WE ARE COMPLETE

Gratitude comes from what *is*, not what might be. That doesn't mean we must abandon our needs and wants, our wishes, hopes, and dreams. But we don't need to wait for external success to arrive before we give thanks for what we already have. Our imagination and enthusiasm can achieve great things in the external world—for us and for others—but we don't need achievements to make us complete; we *are* complete.

We can always choose to accept things *as they are*, experience them *as they are*, and appreciate them *as they are*. When we truly appreciate what is, our gratitude is infinite. Our contentment cannot be measured. Our joy cannot be measured. Our love cannot be measured. Our understanding cannot be measured. Our happiness cannot be measured. Our inner peace cannot be measured. We can't run a tape along their dimensions, like a tailor, and call out the numbers of their shape. We can't put them on the weighing scales. They are infinite and formless but utterly real for us.

When we value every breath, this is reality. When we fully connect with the peace inside us, this is reality. All of this can only happen in the here and now. What is the good karma for "now"? The good karma for now is consciousness. The good karma for now is joy. The good karma for now is gratitude.

BEYOND SUFFERING,
BEYOND SUCCESS

Quite often I'm asked: "What about the bad things happening in my life? Do I need to give gratitude for *them*?" Or as someone once asked me, rather angrily, "Should we be thankful for the confusion? Should we be thankful for the suffering? Should we be thankful for the pain?" No, but in those feelings there is also a sign pointing toward something good—life itself. Without life, you can feel neither the bad nor the good. Without life, you can't be angry, you can't be in pain. Without life, you don't get the opportunity to see the bad times turn good. Here's a story about that.

A King, his Minister, and his Knight were on a secret mission to visit another kingdom when the King cut his thumb while cutting up an apple. It started to bleed heavily, but the Knight put a bandage on it and they continued on. The King was unhappy that he'd been injured and he started to ask himself, over and over: "Why did this happen?" A few miles down the track he turned to his Minister and asked, "Why did I cut myself?"

"Lord, whatever happens, happens for the good," said the Minister.

The King found this pretty irritating, especially as his thumb was throbbing. He thought: "Let's teach him a lesson." So he called over his Knight and told him to find a deep ditch and throw the Minister in it so he couldn't get out.

The Knight did exactly that, although the Minister put

up quite a fight, and even bit the Knight's ear so it bled. The Minister started to yell, "Why are you doing this to me?"

"Well," said the King, "whatever happens, happens for the good."

The King and his Knight left the Minister in the ditch and walked on and on and on until they entered a forest. They walked for hours and then encountered a strange village. Before they knew it, they were surrounded by villagers; the local people were wild with anger at the trespassing visitors. The penalty for coming into their village uninvited was death by sacrifice. The villagers eyed up the King and decided he was the one they would kill first, so they tied him up and started to build a fire.

The King shouted: "This is terrible! Why are they doing this? Save me! Stop!"

The man in charge of the ceremony had begun to make the final preparations when he suddenly turned to the village Chieftain and said: "We cannot sacrifice this man!"

"Why not?" asked the Chieftain.

"Anyone we sacrifice must be perfect, but look at this!" And with that he held up the King's bandaged thumb.

The villagers let out a groan, but they quickly turned their attention to the Knight and tied him up. Once again the person in charge started to make the final preparations, but this time he noticed the Knight's bloody ear.

"We cannot sacrifice this man either!" he shouted, and once again he undid the ropes.

The Chieftain and the villagers were mad with fury. Everyone started to shout and argue. In the chaos, the King and his

Knight were able to quietly slip away. Back through the forest they walked, on and on and on, until they reached the ditch containing the Minister.

"Get him out!" shouted the King. "I'm sorry for throwing you down there; that cut saved my life." And the King told the story of the wild villagers and escaping death.

"And I'm so glad you threw me in the ditch," said the Minister, "because I have no cuts on me, and I would have been sacrificed instead of you!"

This story reminds us about the silver linings that come with the clouds in our life. What does a silver lining tell us? It tells us that there's a powerful sun right behind that dark cloud, waiting to warm us and light our way.

This is not to downplay the impact of the awful things that can happen to us, by the way. I'm simply pointing out that there's always something more than the pain we might be experiencing. And, for that matter, the same is true of pleasure. Everything changes. We may suffer, but suffering does not define us. We may have great success, but success does not define us. Success and suffering may run through our lives, but peace is constant.

Physical pain, mental pain, and emotional pain can overwhelm our mind, but there is always something beautiful happening in our heart. It can be difficult to feel inner peace when you're in the middle of a terrible time, but look within, and there's something beyond suffering to be glimpsed: a gentle reminder that there is joy waiting for you on the other side of pain.

Here are some words from Socrates on this subject:

If you don't get what you want, you suffer; if you get what you don't want, you suffer; even when you get exactly what you want, you still suffer because you can't hold on to it forever. Your mind is your predicament. It wants to be free of change, free of pain, free of the obligations of life and death. But change is a law, and no amount of pretending will alter that reality . . . Life is not suffering, it's just that you will suffer it, rather than enjoy it, until you let go of your mind's attachments and just go for the ride freely, no matter what happens.

THE DARKEST CLOUD

Like anyone, I have good days and I have bad days. But even when it's been a terrible day, I want to be able to turn within and say: "I give thanks that I'm alive." And when I'm having a really terrific day—when everything is going my way—I want to be able to go inside myself and say: "I give thanks that I'm alive." Neither troubles nor happiness should make us forget what's most important. Neither troubles nor happiness need distract us from the peace to be found in our heart.

The darkest cloud that ever blew into my life appeared when I was in Argentina, preparing to speak at an event. I received a phone call telling me that my wife, Marolyn, had been rushed to a hospital. She had been in a hotel in San Diego, with our youngest son, and they'd ordered some pizza from room service. She had bent down to open the room service trolley door when suddenly she passed out and slumped to the floor. Next day, at the hospital, they took a fluid sample from her spine and there was blood, and the test pointed toward something going on with her head. They diagnosed that she'd had an aneurysm in her brain—a serious problem with a blood vessel. I was told there was a substantial risk that she might die.

I put down the phone and looked around me. I was thousands of miles away, in a completely different time zone. That night I was due to address a large crowd of people, many of whom had been waiting years for me to visit their hometown. I was struggling to contain all the information and emotion swirling around in me.

In that moment, I decided to sit down and quietly connect with my self. As I did that, I felt the true weight of the awful events unfolding miles away, but I also felt the peace inside. A great sense of calm and clarity flowed through me. I arranged for our plane to be prepared and, while that was happening, prepared myself to talk to an important audience.

That day, finding a balance between good and bad enabled me to stay on my path. I went to the event and spoke, then left for the airport straight away. I flew through the night, and the whole flight seemed rather surreal. My mind was racing with all the potential consequences of Marolyn's situation, but there was another part of me that was clear about what I needed to do.

We landed, cleared customs, and I went straight to the hospital. Marolyn was awake, but the doctors said it was vital they operated. It was going to be a complex operation. I wanted to be near the hospital, so I checked into a hotel. I stayed there, moving between the hotel and the hospital, for a little over a month. Every day, our family and friends were hanging on to hope. There was always news to process, but I could also feel the strength and simplicity that come from self-knowledge. And that meant I could help Marolyn and the family.

During that time, the whole family was in the depths of suffering, but there was still that gratitude for life itself. We weren't thankful for the problem, but gratitude was still there in us—a light in the darkness, a light that enabled us to keep seeing the full picture of what was going on. After all those days, Marolyn started to mend. Slowly, slowly, slowly. And then she came home, and we took good care of her there. Of course, now you wouldn't know she went through that horrible experience. Our ability to heal—physically, mentally, emotionally—is just extraordinary. (In the next chapter, I talk more about how we can respond to the roughest times in life.)

THE RIVER OF PEACE

I think of inner peace like a river that flows through us. Sometimes we might feel like we're on dry ground, with nothing growing in the earth. There's no texture, no color, no shelter. Then a trickle of peace springs from the hard earth, glistens in the light, and starts to run over the cracked ground, finding the old riverbeds.

As the water bubbles up and moves along the valley, things

happen. Blades of grass begin to grow on the riverbank. Seeds lying in that parched earth sprout and flower. Bugs arrive to eat the grass and the leaves. Bigger bugs want to eat the small bugs, and they attract birds looking for food, and the birds are bringing in all sorts of other seeds, and the seeds fall onto the now fertile ground.

Here come the trees, and the branches are heavy with ripe fruit, and there is every imaginable leaf color and leaf pattern blazing a glorious painting from one side of the horizon to the other, and insect chatter and birdsong fill the air with music. Sweet perfumes float over the vast forest like an invitation for all life to come join the party of joyful creation.

Each plant's and creature's evolution has unique elements, but all of them need water if they are to flourish. Peace is the water that enables life to blossom. I give gratitude for the peace that flows through my life, for the existence I have been blessed with, and for the many colors and patterns of life that bloom for me whenever I connect with myself.

WHAT IS ENOUGH?

I like great food, amazing places, innovative technologies, and all the rest just as much as anyone else. If you're fortunate enough to be relatively prosperous, this world offers some incredible *stuff*. The problem comes when we keep collecting and owning things without *appreciating* them.

Once, I had been at a TV station discussing global problems, and someone had started talking about greed and how they saw it absolutely everywhere. On the way home in the car I began to think about antidotes to greed. Then, when we were stopped at a traffic light, a car pulled up next to ours and the driver had his music blaring out. It was really very loud. Boom. Boom. Boom. Boom. Boom. My first thought was: "That's pretty obnoxious. They don't have to do that." But then I thought again: "Actually, perhaps it's because they like that song so much that they want everyone to hear it!" Maybe that person was just appreciating the song. Then it occurred to me that the antidote to greed is appreciation. And when we truly appreciate something, we want to share it. The opposite is when we covet something and keep it to ourselves.

So, greed is the feeling that we cannot be happy until we get more, but when we start appreciating it, we move closer to a sense of fulfillment. As soon as we fully connect with that feeling of gratitude, it's the end of greed.

We need to be honest with ourselves and recognize what we actually prioritize each day. Is the appreciation of life itself at the very top of our list of what's most important, or does it keep getting pushed further down and down and down by other priorities, until we don't even see it anymore? Relationships, home, career, vacations, events, hobbies, technology, and all the rest—do they really deserve to be higher up our list than experiencing the gift of life itself? I feel we need to prioritize the experience of our blessing, not let it become hidden beneath everything else. What would our life look like if we brought appreciation for this blessing right up top—every single day? How might it change the way we go about things? What do you think it would do for your life?

I see people who are heading to the end of their time here, and they know it, but still their mind keeps putting everything else on top of that priority list. Where is the sincere and profound enjoyment of these precious days that grace our lives? Do we really have bigger priorities than that? The more our mind searches for fulfillment out there in the world, the further we get from the sense of true fulfillment within. Here is some wisdom on this from the poet Kabir:

> The fish in the water is thirsty and every time I see that it makes me laugh.

When we are greedy, we are that fish feeling thirsty in the water. Water, water everywhere, not a drop to drink. We have everything we need but we don't appreciate it. Gratitude for what we have quenches our thirst.

DO YOU FEEL SUCCESSFUL?

Ultimately, everything in the external world is temporary and can leave you at any time, just like that. It's what you *feel* you are, right now, that really counts. Do you feel successful? Only you can decide. Do you feel successful? Only you can create the success you want. Do you feel successful? What does your answer tell you about your connection to yourself?

Do you know how many billions of people will work extremely hard in their life to hear someone else say: "You are successful"? Do you know how many billions of people will dream about the arbitrary line that somebody else has drawn that declares, "This is success"?

Is this what life is, or is there something more? Well, there is an inner world, and in that world you don't need to strive for what others tell you is success; you can simply find it within you. You don't need to strive for fame; you can simply feel loved for who you are. You don't need to strive for other people's respect; you can appreciate who you are. You don't need to weigh and measure your possessions; you can keep unwrapping the gift of life instead.

WANTS AND NEEDS

One reason for our confusion about fulfillment is that we don't always know the difference between our needs and our wants.

Air—maybe three minutes without it and we're a goner.

Warmth—maybe three hours without it and we're a goner.

Water, food, sleep—we need those too.

French fries—that's a want.

Going to that must-see new movie—that's a want.

Buying that shiny new car—that's a want.

There's nothing wrong with wants. They add pleasure to our lives, and they keep the money circulating and people in jobs. What you like today you may not like tomorrow. That's the nature of desire. If desire doesn't change, it's pointless. It constantly shifts. You buy a new TV, and by the time you bring it home, plug it in, and turn it on, it's advertising a new TV. And you then desire that. You go to a restaurant with a friend; you look at the menu and, after careful deliberation, you order your dish. And when the food arrives, you look at your friend's food and you desire that. That's desire: never satisfied!

We end up giving lots of attention to our wants while forgetting about our needs. That's hardly surprising: there's a very noisy multibillion-dollar *want* industry and it's constantly advertising all those things you might want next.

Have you heard that phrase about relationships, "familiarity breeds contempt"? It suggests we can become complacent about people when we spend lots of time with them. It's often the same with the essentials in our life. How many of us woke up this morning and gave thanks for having air, water, food, and warmth? And for having slept?

In my view, it's OK to want *more* of anything, but we have to ensure that it's not at the expense of making something else *less* in our lives. Is there a cost to wanting this thing, or is it simply adding something pleasurable? If it's adding something good, and not subtracting something good, then great!

I'm always impressed when someone has the determination

and focus needed to make material life better for them and their family, especially if they live in a place with harsh economic conditions. But, wherever you are, it's good to keep a balance. I think the trick is for us to keep improving our lot without losing touch with the pure wonder of existence. The wealth of the world can sometimes fulfill our wants, but it's the wealth of our heart that fulfills our needs.

Maybe you've guessed where I'm going next . . . So, is inner peace a want or a need? I once asked that of an audience, and they felt quite confronted; they had to think really hard. Whether feeling connected with inner peace is a want or a need is up to each of us to decide. But I know what inner peace is for me: a deep need. It's not something I look to turn off and on, like air conditioning. It's more like air itself, in fact. None of us think to ourselves: "I don't need to breathe between the hours of nine o'clock in the evening and six in the morning."

The peace needs to dance in us all the time, not just when we sit down and focus on it. Without peace, everything we try to do to make ourselves content won't work; with peace, we have what's vital for our well-being. The point is to thrive, not just survive.

Some people really struggle to get this concept of peace as a need. My sense is that if inner peace is only an intellectual idea in your life—something you are happy to switch off and on according to circumstances—you're probably stuck in believing, not knowing. But it only takes a moment to recognize the treasure within. That feeling of gratitude is just a heartbeat away.

WHO IS CONTENT?

When we're not in touch with the peace inside us, our mind can take us on long journeys of distraction. We can become so unsettled that nothing seems to be quite right in our life. We project fantasies onto other people's lives and stop seeing the blessings in our own.

When this happens, we start to drown in a sea of expectations, and each expectation brings more disappointment, and each disappointment leads to more expectations, and on it goes. In the words of Kabir, "The cow doesn't give milk anymore but you're expecting butter." There is no point having expectations of something that's incapable of fulfilling them.

Benjamin Franklin—that all-around genius—once wrote: "Who is wise? He that learns from everyone. Who is powerful? He that governs his passions. Who is rich? He that is content. Who is that? Nobody."

That "Nobody" makes me smile. It's a wry comment on the human condition. But here I disagree with Franklin: when we make our self the center of our life, we *can* experience true success, we *can* feel fulfillment, we *can* experience deep contentment. All of us. And it starts with gratitude for what we have.

This reminds me of a story I once heard, and I'm going to end the chapter by sharing this tale about a stonecutter and his search for fulfillment.

There was a man, a stonecutter by profession. Every day he would go to the mountain, cut some rocks, and carry them back home. In his workshop he would create little idols, bowls, and so on, and this is how he made his living.

He was unhappy because it was a lot of hard work to go to the mountain, cut the rock, and bring it home. When he was working, there was dust everywhere, and he had to rely on rich people to buy his wares. He felt he had no power, so he was dissatisfied.

One day he was going past the house of a rich man. There was a party going on, and people were eating and drinking. He thought to himself: "I want a good, easy life, not this cutting of stone every day!" He looked up and said: "God, please make me like that."

That day God was listening. (As you may have noticed, He or She doesn't always listen, but that day the stonecutter was in luck.) Boom! Just like that, the stonecutter was transformed into a rich man with a big house and lots of everything that goes with that lifestyle.

"This is it!" he thought to himself. "People bow in front of me, pay respect to me, wait for my command." He was very happy.

One day he happened to see the King passing by. Wealthy people were standing by the road paying their homage to the King, and everybody trembled at his name. The guy thought: "Wow, that's power!" He had been happy until then, but then he wanted more, so he said: "God, I want to be the King." That day too, God was listening. So the man who had been a stonecutter and a rich man then became a King.

One summer morning the man who was now a King

walked out onto his veranda. The sun was shining and every-body, as far as he could see, was trying to hide from its pow-erful rays. "So," he thought, "the sun is more powerful than me! Everybody is taking heed of that sun." And that day too, God was listening when he said: "God, I want to be the sun."

Next moment, there he was, shining in the sky. "This is more like it," he thought. "Everybody is below me, nobody is above me. I control everybody's life. Without me nobody can see. Everybody gets up after I get up. And everybody goes to sleep when I go to sleep. Life is good."

Every day the man who was now a sun would shine, feel-ing his power, until one day a colossal cloud parked itself over his old kingdom. He was trying to shine through the cloud but couldn't. "Hmm, could it be that this cloud is more pow-erful than me? God, I want to be the cloud."

So, there he was, a huge cloud in the sky. He thought: "Now I have true power: I can block out the sun." But one day, to his great amazement, he started to move. "What's making me move?" he wondered. And he realized it was the wind. "The wind is more powerful than me? That can't be allowed!" he thought. "God, I want to be the wind."

Now he was the wind, and he blew and blew, and he rel-ished his power. Then, one day, he was blowing and blowing and he couldn't move anything: "What's more powerful than the wind?" he wondered. It was the biggest mountain he'd ever seen, and it had completely stopped the wind from mov-ing anything.

"God, make me a mountain," he asked. Boom! And he

became the mountain. "*Now* I'm truly the most powerful thing," he thought. "The wind can move the cloud, the cloud that can hide the sun, the sun that is more powerful than the King, the King who is more powerful than the rich man, who is more powerful than the stonecutter. But the wind cannot move mountains, and now I am the biggest mountain. This is it!"

He was happy for some time, then, one day, he heard a tap-tap-tapping noise. It felt like somebody was cutting a part of him away. "Who can be so powerful that they can cut into the mountain?" he thought. "This must be the most powerful person on Earth." He looked down and saw that it was a stonecutter.

CHAPTER 7

Unburden for Rough Times

A patient went to the doctor and said: "Doctor, it hurts everywhere."

The doctor said: "What do you mean, 'It hurts everywhere'?"

"When I touch myself here, it hurts; when I touch myself here, it hurts; when I touch myself here, it hurts. All over my body, it hurts."

"I know what's wrong," replied the doctor. "You have a broken finger."

When you're experiencing life's pain, *everything* can feel like it's a source of suffering. Rough times cast a bad light on the world around you. A gorgeous sunset, a party packed with old friends, dinner at your favorite restaurant: what might normally be a source of delight can become a reminder of all that feels wrong in your life. Everything hurts.

I know that pain. I know there are no easy answers when life gets difficult. Sometimes it seems like we are going forward. Sometimes it seems like we are going backward. Some days are easy and some days are rough. Some days are *very* rough. But as the old saying goes, "Pain is inevitable, suffering is optional."

For me, there's a helpful distinction to be made between tough times and rough times. Life can throw all sorts of tough times at us. The problems involved aren't always easy to solve, but deep down we sense we can do something about them—we *can* change our situation. In the rough times, however, we might feel things are hopeless and there's little or nothing we can do. These occasions hit our courage hard, and it may feel as if emotions like fear, frustration, regret, and sorrow have taken over our lives.

Sometimes there really isn't anything we can do to change our situation. Some aspects of life are beyond our control, and we need to be realistic about that. But we do always have a choice about how we respond *within* ourselves. The rough times may distance us from our clarity and wisdom, but those strengths are always there within us. Even recognizing that we have the choice to connect with our inner strengths can be the start of a turnaround in how we feel.

As we move through life's difficulties, two realities exist side by side: the bad that's going through our mind and the good that's forever in our heart. We always have that possibility to connect with the good inside, if we choose to. Even in the roughest times.

Here, I share some more thoughts that might lighten the

emotional darkness that can accompany the rough times in your life. I want to start by making a positive case for the good in humankind, because there is no darkness greater than believing you are what's wrong with this world.

HAVE YOU HEARD THE NEWS?

It's incredible, the sheer volume of information that we can now access through our TV and other devices. We have the potential to be very well informed. But news also exposes us to some of the most disturbing things happening in our neighborhood and beyond. A story becomes news because it's unusual, so if we keep consuming more and more negative news, our sense of reality can become distorted. Then the world feels like an increasingly dangerous place and people can seem mostly bad.

Now, awful things do happen in the world, but soaking up every bad news story and wringing our hands helps no one and makes us miserable. Instead, we can put our energy into empathizing with those affected by terrible events and taking direct action to help them if we can. We can also question what role, if any, *we* have in the situation. Are we part of the problem in some way? And we must always remember that there's much more love, compassion, and generosity in this world than hate—all the good news that never gets reported.

If you still doubt that your species has the capacity for good, then you really are experiencing a rough time. Here's a suggestion: look hard within and find the good in *you* before you give attention to the good and bad in others. Find the inner strengths in *you*. Find the love in *you*. However far someone else may have strayed from the starting point of peace, there is always the possibility they can return. And the same is true for us, of course. An abandoned field has the potential to become a beautiful garden. Peace *is* possible.

WHEN OUR LOVED ONES DIE

One of the most profoundly difficult times we go through is when someone we love passes away. It can leave us with so many unanswered questions, with a deep sense of emptiness, with numbness, anger, and confusion.

Each person is unique in the way they feel their pain. We pass through stages of grief, sometimes returning to each feeling as our mind and heart reshape themselves. I've seen people move through a period of mourning and then return straight back to being their old self, while others emerge with their life profoundly changed. I've also known people to feel emotionally shattered for many years.

I have no simple remedy for the worst moments of loss and sorrow, just some observations that may help. In my own experience, once my initial feelings of grief have settled, I look to understand how my relationship with that person has changed—not ended, but changed. It can take time to realize that your loved one has physically left their body. But of course, if they're not there in the body, they must be somewhere else. And where they're *always* going to be is with you—in your heart.

Memories cannot replace the person that lived, in all of their many qualities: the scent of their skin, the song of their voice, their eyes when laughing, their warmth on a cold night. But the best of your loved one lives on in your memories of them. You carry this new form of them wherever you go. For me, I want the joyous memories of the person I've lost to dance within me.

I was eight and a half years old when my father passed away. I was very attached to him. He was very loving but quite strict. People had great reverence for him, but when you're a child, you just accept things as they are, so this was all normal for me—he was simply my father. Thousands would gather to hear him speak, and those events were magical. Everyone had come with one purpose, which was to know a little more about themselves. He would sit down and start talking, and from that moment there would be absolute silence. I was very fortunate to be a part of it. To experience just one day of that in a lifetime would be very special, but I lived it for a number of years.

In the first few days after my father passed, I didn't really understand what had happened. I just remember crying and crying. And then, after a while, I realized something: in my heart I could still see him, hear him, feel him. It's been quite a few years since then, but I still see him and I still hear him and I still feel him in me. When somebody passes away, there is nothing you can do about it. All you *can* do is begin to accept. Then, slowly perhaps, you can begin to understand that they are with you in a new way. That feeling of connection can never be taken from you.

Many, many people felt great sadness when my father passed away. Some days later a large crowd gathered, and I could see that people were very upset. I didn't want them to keep feeling such grief, and suddenly I found myself walking onto the stage and up to the microphone. I looked out at those faces and said: "There's no need to cry. The one you're crying for is still here with us in our hearts, in your being, and he always will be." When people heard this sentiment from me, it was very uplifting for them, and they started cheering. Perhaps they could see an aspect of my father in me, but they could also feel his energy in *them*.

Just as energy cannot be destroyed, only transformed or transferred, so our loved ones become something else, somewhere else. This is how Nature works. This is how universal power moves. Constant evolution. A seed transforms into a tree, and that tree gives fruit, and each one of the fruits has a seed, and each one of the seeds has the potential to become another tree. When you hold a seed, what do you have in your hand? Something tiny, but also the possibility of a forest. Feel the forest in the seed.

Your loved one will always be present in you. Their energy is passed on through you. And they are always part of that infinite universal energy that is consciousness. Open your heart and you can sense their presence.

LOOK UP TO THE MOON

Many scientists believe the Moon came from Earth. The theory (sometimes called the giant impact hypothesis) is that a gigantic body smashed into our young planet, and a fabulous new satellite was formed from the debris. Some refer to this body as Theia, naming it after the mother of Selene, the moon goddess, in Greek myth. So the Moon may be part Earth and part Theia.

When the Moon left us, it only went so far. Now it orbits its old home and, as it moves, influences us down here. Perhaps we could think of our passed loved one becoming our Moon. They are always part of us. They circle our life. They illuminate our nights. They pull on the tides of our emotions, moving us. Look up and see the reflection of light from the Sun on their face.

We can honor the person who passed and accept them in the new way they are with us. There's no need to hold on to what was. We can float on the tide of life, letting the water support us as we gaze up into the night sky and feel the connection with that Moon. We can sense our pain while also knowing there is a life-long feeling of togetherness with them in our heart. We can treasure what *was* by celebrating what *is*: carrying our loved ones through life in our love.

Here's a poem by me about the way we can keep our loved ones with us, and the strength that brings:

Just as the night seems heavy with darkness
So the moon rises and starts to glow
There will be a little light for you
Not only to admire
But also to see by.

TO REST WITHIN YOURSELF

Is there a rougher challenge for us than losing someone we love? For some, it's the dark thought that one day they are going to die. People can encounter fear of their own end at different stages of their life. This fear may press especially close if we become very ill or are in a dangerous situation, but it can haunt us even when we are safe and well.

I'm often asked to speak to someone facing death. Although it can feel counterintuitive, I find it helpful to first acknowledge the reality of our mortality. We must all understand that, ultimately, we each have to go. It's a fantasy to think the life you have now can last forever. But exactly *when* are you going to go? Nobody can tell you! What do you really know about your life and death? The only thing you know for sure is that you were born and you're alive right now, in this moment.

When we're ill, it really helps to remember that we have incredible strength deep inside us. We need to find those friends and use them if we can, to put all the positive energy we have inside us to work. Serious illness (and grief, disappointment, anxiety, and all our other negative experiences and feelings) can distance us from our courage—and from our clarity, our fulfillment, our joy, and our peace. But our courage *is* still there within. Our clarity *is* still there within. Our fulfillment *is* still there within. Our joy *is* still there within. Our peace *is* still there within. Through the rough times, we always have access to the resources in our hearts.

There's a quality about peace that I'd really like to express: it enables you to rest within yourself. When the outside world pushes you to your limits, know that you can always connect with something unchangeable and sustaining within. When you have been wearied by the battles of life, know that you can rest within. As my father said about the sensation of going deep inside and experiencing your self: it's like being asleep without sleeping. When we need to, we can head away from the noise and into that nourishing feeling of inner peace.

GREAT EXPECTATIONS

One way we can help ourselves through the rough times—in fact, through any time, good or bad—is to notice how expectations shape our experience. Every day I have expectations. I have expectations of my alarm clock. I have expectations when I pick up a saltshaker that there's going to be salt in it. It's fine to set expectations, as long as we keep understanding that they don't always match reality. As the boxer Mike Tyson put it, rather bluntly, "Everyone has a plan until they get punched in the mouth."

It takes courage to accept life as it really is, rather than getting distracted by fear or fantasy. Clarity about what *is* can save us from a great deal of heartache. Or as Seneca expressed it, "We suffer more in imagination than in reality."

What happens when you become led by expectations? Well, you can probably get over the disappointment of an empty saltshaker. I know a few people who would have a meltdown if their electronics stopped working, but they'd survive. The real problems start with other people and the expectations we project onto one another. There can be a tremendous amount of anger and sadness generated by unfulfilled wishes. Relationships fall apart. It can be a mess.

There was once a young farmer who had to transport his heavy bags of produce to the market by hand each week. It was tough work, and he was limited by how much he alone could carry, so he saved hard to buy a donkey. His wife disagreed. She said that what they needed was a cow, because the cow would give them milk and butter. They got a young cow. His misery at having to carry heavy bags to the market did not diminish, but he kept working hard until they had enough money to get a donkey. The donkey transformed his life. The problem was that there was very little space in their yard, and before long the cow was fully grown, and the donkey was now the one feeling miserable. In fact, the donkey was now in danger of being crushed.

The man grew frustrated with this state of affairs and prayed to God: "Lord, this can't go on: please will you kill the cow? Then my donkey can have the space he needs." Next morning he awakens to find the donkey has died. "Oh Lord," he says, "I thought by now you would know the difference between a cow and a donkey."

Expectations!

Think of some of the weddings you've been to or have heard about. As soon as you realize the happy couple or the families are hoping for "the perfect wedding," you know there's going to be trouble. The first thing a friend or a wedding planner should say to those planning a wedding is this: "Nothing ever goes entirely to plan!"

Of course, it's great to set exciting expectations about important areas of our life—relationships, house, job, family weddings—we just shouldn't cling to them. Disappointment robs the moment of its wonder. We waste far too much of our precious life regretting that the actual now didn't measure up to our idea of it. So what's at fault when that happens: reality or our imagination? If we're rigid in our approach, we feel the impact of unexpected events and disappointments even more. We become stronger when we learn to flex with what is. Think of the way a tree sways with the wind. Think of the way a bird flies in a storm. Think of the way fish move with the tide.

Who sets our expectations? We do! We are the ones who create our own expectations. We are the ones who accept other people's expectations. Sometimes an expectation is met, sometimes it isn't. The point is this: other people may put expectations on us, but we don't have to make them our own. When we feel disappointed, we often feel disappointed with ourselves. And that strikes me as a waste of our precious time.

WHY DON'T YOU LOOK LIKE YOU?

It takes a lot to stand back from your thoughts and see how wedded you are to a particular outcome. It's like an obstinate person who gets lost: they prefer to believe their interpretation of the map rather than the world they see around them, until they're forced to recognize something really has gone wrong. And then they blame the map. We get caught in the trap of following our mind, even when our heart is telling us that something isn't quite right.

I once arrived at a big speaking event, and some of the organizers were waiting by the stage-door area so they could escort me inside from the car. They had seen me speak many times before, and I appreciated that they wanted to welcome me in this way.

That day I wasn't wearing a tie or a suit, which was unusual for me when going to an event. It was a long drive, so I probably decided to dress comfortably for the journey. When my car pulled up, the welcome party just stood there looking at us. They didn't move. Then I opened my door and started to get out. "No, no, no!" they shouted. "Move the car! Move the car! We're expecting someone at any moment! Move the car!"

They were staring straight at me, but I realized each one of them was looking for the suit and tie. Take those away, and the rest of me didn't register with their *expectation*. And then one of them saw reality and was embarrassed. "Oh! We're so sorry, we didn't realize it was you!" The others kept looking at me as if to say: "Why don't you look like you?"

AN AGE-OLD PROBLEM

"He who is of a calm and happy nature will hardly feel the pressure of age, but to him who is of an opposite disposition, youth and age are equally a burden." So declared the Greek philosopher Plato (who lived into his early eighties, by the way). As I get older, I appreciate those words more each time I read them. Aging is a complex business, and it can be a severe test of character.

Our ego certainly takes a knock along the way. But so much of what fills our minds about getting older is fear-driven noise. "I can't do that, I'm sixty years old, you know!" OK, so maybe you *can't* run a marathon anymore—or perhaps your marathon time is now over five hours. Either way, big deal!

Whatever your age, there are some things you can no longer do, some you can't do as well, and many new things you *can* now do. Embrace what is and forget what can't be. Much of aging is in our mind. In our youth, we love life and don't care about death. When we become afraid to both live and die, that's when we're old.

GET REAL

You were cooking your dinner, you went to do something, and now everything is burned. That was the only food in the house and it's too late to go shopping. I'm sure you've been in this or a similar situation. Just as you're thinking through what's happening, someone pipes up: "Be positive!"

Well, here's the truth: I'm not feeling positive—there's no food to eat! What I need to be is realistic, not positive. Which brings me to this point: my messages about the solace of inner peace and the need to seize the day are not simply invitations to "be positive!" I'm not saying whitewash every bad situation with grinning optimism. Instead, we can appreciate and enjoy life more if we see the world and understand ourselves clearly. The rough times you experience are real, but the joy within you is real too. The rough times you experience are real, but the peace within you is real too. Living consciously means being as realistic as possible about any situation—in the world around you *and* the world inside you. Feel disappointment, feel grief, feel anger, feel loneliness, feel depression: acknowledge the pain, but also know you can always choose to connect with the peace inside.

A great Chinese proverb states: "Don't blame God for having created the tiger; thank him for not giving it wings." Imagine the havoc a winged tiger could wreak! Fortunately, we don't have to deal with such imaginary creatures, and we don't have to deal with imaginary situations, either. I've found that life gets easier if we focus on dealing with what *is*. Reality is the best place to live.

Being realistic can help us prepare for what's to come next in our lives. If you're having a good time, be aware that bad times are coming—at some point. No need to worry, just know. If you're having a bad time, be aware good times are coming at some point. No need to project your mind into every possible future scenario; just know change is coming and feel your resilience.

As part of being realistic, we can know that—even in the wildest storms of our life—there is a place that is very calm, and that place is within us. This is what I know: I can be in peace within myself both in moments that are wonderful and moments that are terrible. I cannot always escape or sail through life's storms, but I can go to a place of calm within me.

So, I have a positive frame of mind but I'm a realist. When I pilot a plane, I *always* take extra fuel. When you're learning to fly, you hear this advice: "Three things are useless to you in an emergency: the runway behind you, the sky above you, and the fuel in the truck." If you've used up most of the runway and not taken off, all that runway behind you isn't going to do you any good. If you've lost power and you're coming in for an emergency landing, it's how much air you have below you that's critical, not all that sky up there. And the fuel sitting in the truck at the airport is no good to you once you're in the air. That's being realistic.

BECOMING THE PILOT OF YOUR LIFE

I heard a story when I was in Florida learning to fly helicopters that always makes me laugh. It's a good reminder of how we can sometimes become the creator of our own problems, our own rough times. I should preface it by saying that pilots are prone to telling tall tales or embellishing the details of a story. This one is based on real events, but there's probably some added color in places!

There was a guy who had one of those small airplanes where you have to take the propeller and spin it by hand to get it started. One day, he went to do that, and nothing happened. There was no power and the propeller didn't move. So, he got inside the cockpit and increased the throttle, which put more power into the engine—just like when you're trying to start up an old car. Then he tried again, but that didn't work either. So he added some more throttle. And then some more.

Finally, the pilot spun the propeller hard and the engine burst into life, but he had given it so much throttle that the plane started to really power up. Now it wanted to move, which was good, but he was standing outside the cockpit, which was very bad! The man had put a big chock in front of *one* of the wheels so the plane wouldn't shift position, but the other wheel didn't want to stand still and started to move. So one wheel was stuck and the other wheel was free, which meant the plane began to go around in a circle. Then it gained speed.

At this point the pilot tried to grab a strut on a wing,

but doing that made the other wheel jump over its block. So now there was nothing stopping the plane from moving off down the runway other than him clinging on. He just couldn't hold it forever, probably because he was getting dizzy going round and round. When he finally let go, the airplane straightened itself out, headed toward the runway picking up speed, went down and up a dip, and then took off—with no pilot inside.

Nearby, there were some other pilots training on helicopters, and they had seen what happened, so they started to chase the plane. Imagine that scene flying over you—an air chase. The empty plane was just happily flying along, oblivious to everything else, doing what it was designed to do. It flew like that for about an hour and forty-five minutes until it ran out of fuel, stalled, and started a slow descent before performing the gentlest of crash landings on open ground. The helicopter pilots were all amazed at the smooth way that plane flew.

The reason this story comes to mind is that sometimes it's the *pilot* who crashes an airplane. They get into the cockpit and think: "OK, I've got to do *this*, and I've got to do *this*, and I've got to do *this*," and their actions cause the problems. Left alone, the plane in the story did its job wonderfully well while it was in the air, with nobody in it. When you're flying, you need to give the plane guidance that's productive and realistic, letting it do what it's designed for and no more. In life it's like that too. If we constantly think, "Well, I must make my life do *this* for me, and *this*, and *this*," you can come crashing down to Earth. There's a beautiful simplicity to life if we let it do what it's designed to do.

When things go wrong in our life, we tend to blame other people, or bad fortune, or karma. Sometimes, however, it's down to how we're handling ourselves. Do we have clarity? Do we have realistic plans? Are we flexing in response to unexpected conditions? Are we trying to make our life perform in a way that it can't, rather than allow it to do what it does best? In my experience, we want to try to get the balance right between controlling our life and letting it flourish—between guiding the plane and letting it fly.

FIND YOUR FIRE

There is a proverb that says: "It is better to light a candle than curse the darkness." You can lay in your bed all night long and curse that darkness, but it won't bring light. We can sit down in the dark forest of our problems and weep—and I do know that problems can seem overwhelming at times—but at some point we have to say: "Enough is enough."

In that situation, we need to summon up our courage, strike a match, and light that candle. Then we can use the flame from that candle to light another candle. Guess what? The light of the first candle doesn't go out: we have twice the light. And we can keep going until we illuminate our life again. But only a lit candle can light other candles, so we always need to find that fire within us.

And what is the light? It is consciousness: the one true light that can guide us through life. Even in the roughest times.

My perspective on the rough times isn't new, but the message is as relevant today as I imagine it was back in the days of Plato, or when the poet Kabir was writing in the fifteenth century, or thousands of years before either of them. My points are simple: the world can be a difficult place, but people are born good, and peace can be found in everyone. Death takes what we love and transforms it into something we can still feel and honor. Staring reality square in the eye takes courage but liberates us to experience life as it actually is. We must rule over our expectations or they will rule over us. And during both the roughest of days and the loveliest of days, we always have that possibility to connect inside with our true self—to *choose* to experience the joy, fulfillment, and peace within our heart.

These themes remind me of a poem by Kabir.

Gleaming light of the moon sparkles within
Blind eyes cannot bathe in it
Within is the moon and the sun
And within is the silent sound
Within play all the instruments in harmony
The deaf ears hear not even a word of the song
If you keep to my and mine
You won't succeed in a single task
When I am no longer attached to mine
Then my beloved comes to finish my task

Desire to be free, one gains Knowledge
Yet only after self-knowledge are you truly free
For the plants desire to have fruit, the flowers bloom
Once the fruit is ready the plant does not need
    the flowers anymore
Like the musk deer carries the musk within its navel
The deer searching for the scent does not search within itself,
    but rather the grass

All the instruments within you are playing in harmony. Listen to the peace deep inside. This is the silent sound. Listen closely, and perhaps you can hear yourself.

CHAPTER 8

Free Yourself Through Forgiveness

Imagine a world where everyone lives in peace. Imagine what would spring from that global peace—the beautiful flowers of kindness. Imagine a world where society uses its talents, resources, and energy for the good of all. Where the many, many billions of dollars currently spent on defense are used instead to attack disease rather than each other. Where communities and families aren't fractured by violence and crime but are united, strong, understanding, and caring. Where everyone's home is safe, comfortable, and welcoming. Where new technologies are designed to serve humankind, helping us prosper. Where there is plentiful food and water, and we happily share what we have with friends, neighbors, and strangers. Where borders are no more than lines on old maps. Where creatures of every shape and size have space to thrive. Where Nature is loved and respected. Where our villages, towns, and cities overflow with gratitude and generosity.

Imagine that world.

Instead of looking down the barrel of the gun of destruction, we could live like this—in peace. All of us. As one.

"Yes!" we say. "This is what we want!" But such an ideal world will never happen unless, first, we truly understand what peace is. Very few do. We know all about war but very little about peace.

We may have many ideas about peace, but often they are little more than utopian dreams. And what does the name "utopia" mean? In Greek *ou* means "no" and *topos* means "place"—so, together: "no place." We are dreaming of a place that can never exist unless we start to look for it in a different way. Peace is to be found within you—this is the message that has echoed through the centuries. It starts within *your* self and within *my* self.

We can only begin to know what peace is when we experience inner peace for ourselves, hence the importance of self-knowledge. When we understand the peace inside us, and get in touch with that peace, *then* we can understand what peace is between people. *Then* we can choose to be truly peaceful in the way we act. *Then* the global peace we're looking for has a chance of becoming a reality rather than existing only in the form of an abstract "utopia."

JUST ONE SEED

I find conversations about peace can produce all sorts of ifs, buts, and maybes relating to "other people." We ask: If other people don't want to live in peace, how can we make global peace possible? Personal peace sounds great, but how do we get all the other people in society to follow our example? Maybe other people are the problem, not the solution?

Our focus on "other people" distracts us from looking within. True, inspiring billions of individuals to fully embrace peace is a huge task, but there's a good way to begin: one person at a time. And who is the person we have to start with? Ourselves!

Picture you and me standing in a vast field, with more and more fields stretching all around to the horizon. I say: "I want you to create a forest in this field and in every surrounding field too." You say: "OK, that sounds like a great idea!" But how will you begin?

It seems like an enormous and complicated challenge—virtually impossible—but really it's very simple if you understand the nature of a tree. Each tree has the potential to multiply itself. All you need to start is healthy earth and the right seed, because one tree can propagate a forest. There's no need to plant 10,000 tree seeds by hand. No need to bring in water, heavy equipment, experts, and so on. None of that is necessary if you have fertile ground and one seed. Just one seed.

LEARNING TO CHOOSE

Are there times when it is legitimate for us to fight, even to go to war? Perhaps. It is up to each of us to choose war or peace for ourselves, according to what we feel in our heart. We have both war and peace within us, and there is both clarity and confusion in us too. We can only make the right choice when we understand ourselves.

In a famous part of that great Sanskrit epic the *Mahabharat*, the god Krishna accompanies Arjun, a warrior, on the battlefield. What happens next tells us something significant about peace and war, partly because our hero, Arjun, makes a surprising decision.

So, a great battle is set to begin, and Arjun says he does not want to fight. He looks around at the ranks of soldiers and he sees a long line of family members, friends, teachers, comrades. He has no desire to pick up his bow against those he loves and knows. His reasons seem noble and selfless.

Now, you might think that Krishna would be pleased by Arjun embracing peace. Not so. Why? Because Arjun lacks self-knowledge. The warrior has not understood the many factors that should shape his decision. His sentiments are utopian, and he has not seen the whole picture. His feelings aren't connected to the reality of his situation. Put another way, he doesn't truly know himself.

Krishna talks to Arjun, explaining the background to the battle and helping him understand his place within the world, including his duty as a warrior to take part in a righteous war. Slowly, the warrior understands his position, then he realizes that he's now completely free to choose for himself. It's making the right choice that's important, and that starts with knowing you *have* a choice.

Say you are in prison and for many years you've been looking out from your cell window, plotting an escape. There is a high wall very close to you and that's all you see. It dominates your view, barely letting any light into your cell. You think this is the only wall that separates you from freedom, but some way behind that wall is another wall. The second wall is even higher than the first wall, but the wall closer to your cell blocks your view of that second wall. Beyond that second wall is a wall higher still, but you can't see that third wall either because of the first wall.

For weeks you have been secretly gathering all the equipment needed to scale the first wall. Once again, you measure your ropes carefully and decide you have enough to scale the wall. You break out of your cell and quickly climb to the top of the wall. But on top of the first wall you're faced with the second wall, and your ropes won't reach the top of that wall. You have misunderstood your situation.

Unless we see the whole picture, we cannot make the right decision. Unless we have self-knowledge, we cannot connect to the peace in our heart. Unless we are connected to the peace in our heart, we may choose to fight for the wrong reasons. And unless we are connected to the peace in our heart, we may choose to not fight for the wrong reasons. From inner peace comes the clarity to choose. Instead of dreaming about utopia, we need to see reality clearly and make our choice.

ANOTHER GIANT LEAP

So, is world peace *really* possible? Are we humans actually capable of living together in harmony? Many people think not. The negativity you can encounter around this subject is pretty sobering, actually. Seneca said: "It's not because things are difficult that we dare not venture; it's because we dare not venture that they are difficult." Dare we venture to give peace an opportunity?

I'd like to take you back to something that happened a while ago. It lasted for 12 seconds and covered just 120 feet, but it changed the world. I'm talking about the first powered flight. No doubt many people had looked at the Wright brothers' daring plan and said: "This isn't going to work!" Or: "You're naïve!" Or: "If God meant us to fly, he would have given us wings!" But these two guys, who started out repairing bicycles, had big imaginations. And they didn't understand the word "no." That's called persistence. We need more persistence and more daring when it comes to peace.

There is another example of flight I give to people who say peace is impossible: we went to the moon. Did this mission—this one giant leap from imagination to reality—succeed because of the people who declared: "This cannot be done!" or those who said: "Let's try"? Listen to the ambition in President John F. Kennedy's words from 1962:

We choose to go to the Moon. We choose to go to the Moon in this decade and do the other things, not because they are easy, but because they are hard, because that goal will serve to organize and measure the best of our energies and skills, because that challenge is one that we are willing to accept, one we are unwilling to postpone, and one which we intend to win.

Perhaps we have to unlearn some of the negativity we've taken on board since those first lunar adventures. Making peace a reality here on Earth would surely be our greatest collective achievement, so how about we strengthen our resolve? What if we were to follow Kennedy's lead and say:

We choose to achieve peace between people. We choose to do so in this decade not because it is easy, but because it is hard, because that goal will serve to organize and measure the best of our energies and skills, because that challenge is one that we are willing to accept, one we are unwilling to postpone, and one which we intend to win. Because peace is possible when we each start with ourselves.

THE CURSE OF REVENGE

Conflicts happen when we lose respect for each other. In the absence of respect, our principles and rules become more important than people. The head takes over from the heart, then we start to project concepts onto those we're against. War propagandists have known for centuries that it pays to dehumanize the other side. If you turn your opposition into monsters, it makes it easier for decent people to hate them. A society takes a step on the journey toward peace when it recognizes its enemy as human, and that happens one person at a time.

This brings me to the subject of revenge, of "I have been wronged, I must get even!" That feeling can seem so deeply just, so rooted in being right. Even more than this, it can feel as if you have to exact revenge to protect yourself. But does that do anything other than breed fear, hatred, and a desire for revenge in others?

The narrative of the *Mahabharat* is driven by the Kurukshetra War, a conflict that grew out of a struggle between two groups of cousins—the Kauravs and the Pandavs—who both felt they were the rightful heirs to the ancient Indian kingdom of Kuru. Some believe this war led to the start of Kali Yug, one of the four Yugs, or ages—in Indian mythology, a time when discord, quarreling, and strife take hold.

There's one story about revenge in the *Mahabharat* that has always stayed with me. It captures what happens when we lose our clarity about who we are, especially that connection with the peace inside our heart. And it's also about the importance of choosing well. As with Krishna and Arjun on the battlefield, the original version is a pretty long and complex tale—and much of it is open to interpretation and variation—so I'll summarize as simply as I can.

It is some time after the war, and a nobleman called Parikshit has become King. He is considered a fine ruler and the people are blessed by peace and prosperity. One day, he is out on his horse and he meets Kali Yug, which has taken the form of a person (this is normal in the *Mahabharat*, which is full of personification and metaphor).

Kali Yug stands in front of Parikshit and says: "I am Kali Yug and I want to spread throughout your kingdom—it is my time." And Parikshit says: "I'm not going to allow you to do that because I know who and what you are. You are the very thing that will make people confused, that will make them fight among themselves, and they will forget their responsibilities."

Kali Yug realizes he has quite a challenge here. "How can it be that I am everywhere else but not in *his* kingdom?" he thinks to himself, yet he also knows that Parikshit is a mighty ruler and he dares not challenge him directly. He considers the situation for a moment, then he says: "Listen, I'm asking you for shelter."

Well, it's always the King's duty to provide shelter when asked in this way, so it becomes Parikshit's turn to think fast. "Is there some place I can put him where he won't harm my kingdom?" he wonders. "How can I keep him close so I always have my eye on him?" Then Parikshit says these fateful words: "Okay, you can come and shelter in my mind."

Kali Yug is delighted because he knows from there he can go on to occupy the kingdom.

A few days pass and Parikshit decides to go on a hunt. At

one point he feels thirsty; he sees an ashram and goes inside in search of water. Here he encounters a rishi (a wise man) called Shamika, and he is in deep meditation. Parikshit says to him: "Give me some water, rishi!" But Shamika doesn't hear him. And so the King says: "Please, rishi, I humbly ask you for some water." And Shamika still doesn't respond.

At this point Parikshit gets angry, which is very unusual for him. In fact, he becomes more than just angry: he's feeling belittled. He sees a dead snake nearby and puts the unclean animal around the rishi's neck—a terrible insult.

One of the rishi's disciples sees all this happen and curses the King, saying that he will meet his death by the snake Takshak within seven days. Parikshit realizes his mistake and apologizes to Shamika, but there's nothing he can do to reverse the curse.

A tower is built rapidly to protect the King, and he has his soldiers standing ready to kill any snake that approaches. On the seventh day, Parikshit thinks maybe the curse isn't going to come true. It's just past sunset and he feels hungry, so he reaches for some fruit. As he does so, a worm appears. He jokes that, if it is a snake, he will let it bite him. At which point Takshak transforms himself from the worm into his snake body and fulfills the curse.

Janmijay, Parikshit's son, is outraged. He's so angry he wants to start destroying all the snakes in the kingdom. He organizes a huge Sapt Satra, or snake sacrifice, and his men burn every serpent they can find. And so the cycle of revenge goes on.

In the story, Parikshit, Shamika's disciple, and Janmijay *all* feel they have been victims of injustice. From this feeling comes a rage that burns everything in its path, including their own sense of who they are. Janmijay is finally persuaded to stop the sacrifice by another rishi, Astik. "The snakes still living are virtuous (apart from Takshak, of course) and do not deserve to be destroyed," says Astik. "Your glory will increase if you spare their lives." Janmijay halts the burning.

I'll leave you to find out more about the Kali Yug story, if you're interested, otherwise I'll end up trying to summarize the whole *Mahabharat*! The point is that Kali Yug has come and clarity has gone. What takes hold then? Anger, pain, fear, revenge—repeated over and over. This cycle of horror produces nothing but grief. You can demand an eye for an eye, but—as Gandhi was reputed to have said—that just leaves the whole world blind.

A DIFFERENT PERSPECTIVE ON FORGIVENESS

The path from fury to forgiveness can be steep and difficult, especially when great harm has been done to you and those you love. A breakthrough comes if we can see forgiveness not as meek acceptance but as a courageous way to liberate ourselves from pain.

Some actions are so terrible, so damaging, so cruel, and so hateful that they cannot be accepted. They *must* be met with justice. Forgiveness is about severing the relationship with the historic action so it doesn't keep holding us back. Forgiveness does not set the perpetrator free of responsibility; it sets us free from the perpetrator.

I've met many survivors of conflict, and some of their stories have made me sob. I know that the sons and daughters of those killed in wars can grow up with revenge in their heart. The feelings we carry from such traumatic events are never easy to leave behind, but we take our first steps away from victimhood when we choose to act for ourselves. It is so impressive when a revenge-seeker finds the inner strength to rise above their fear and fury. I've been amazed at people's determination to live well today despite what happened to them in the past. And that's an important point: they suffered, but they do not want to live the rest of their life feeling like a victim.

IN SOUTH AFRICA

I first visited South Africa in 1972, when I was fourteen years old. I went to speak at events there and I was appalled by what I saw and experienced. It reminded me of the terrible caste system in India, which I hated. At that time, Nelson Mandela was in jail for his attempts to overturn the regime.

Apartheid was utterly brutal. On one occasion, the South

African government told me: "You cannot do a mixed event. People of different races have to be kept segregated." And I said: "Sorry, I'm not going to do that. Anybody can come to my events. I talk to human beings. I don't talk to their race. I don't talk to their religion."

I was blacklisted. Government officials didn't want to arrest this young visiting speaker and spark an international news event, but instead they followed and monitored me 24/7. I think I broke just about every one of their rules in terms of where I went, how I traveled, who I mixed with, and what I said. Their fear and anger about that were remarkable.

There was a wonderful collection of humans at my events— every shape, size, and color of person you can imagine—but we were all on the same quest: to feel the peace inside us and live a fulfilled life. This wonderful possibility was being entertained in the face of segregation and violence. It was counter to all the rules of the time, and it showed me how the peace within us is more powerful than the dangerous mind games people sometimes play—games with devastating consequences.

In recent years I've held events in Soweto, a place where people have been hurt like you wouldn't believe. A lot of visiting speakers there talk about forgiveness, but I'm often the only one who talks about forgiveness being first and foremost *for you* rather than *for them,* the perpetrators. I say this: People can commit acts that are so heinous you probably can't forgive them, but there is one thing you can do for yourself: cut the bondage of pain. By doing that you ensure what happened yesterday no longer rules your life today.

Once, in South Africa, I was speaking at an event, and a woman in jail had sent a question for me. It was this: "I have done something in my life that I cannot forgive myself for. I killed two of my own children, and nearly killed myself, because of abuse I was suffering. I want to feel the peace that you are talking about. But I think I have lost the capability to feel it. Is there any chance for me?"

I looked out at the audience. I realized that they were much closer to these awful events than I was. I said to them: "Well, do you think there is any chance for this person?"

It was really very surprising, but everyone—with *one* voice—said: "Yes!" That was their answer—there is hope for her. That moment will stay with me forever. It told me, loud and clear, that there *is* hope for humanity.

DUTY AND RESPONSIBILITY

In the story from the *Mahabharat* I told earlier, Janmijay was challenged by Astik, and he replied that he was fulfilling his duty, his dharm. Some people feel a heavy *moral* obligation to fight—for their country, their religion, their community, their family. I'm not going to try to define what duty you have toward others; I just want to remind you that you also have a duty to yourself. And the duty to yourself is to understand *you* before acting, and to experience the peace in *you* before choosing to fight or not. Your mind may be talked into accepting the justification for war, but what about your heart?

Some years back, the Prem Rawat Foundation took its Peace Education Program (PEP) to Sri Lanka, a country that had endured a terrible civil war. Used initially to help prison inmates, PEP supports a range of people who want to reintegrate with society by helping them understand and reconnect with their personal sense of peace. In Sri Lanka, we worked to help ex-combatants get back in touch with themselves, and this had a powerful impact. A former Tamil Tiger said to me: "If I had known this message earlier in my life, I would never have gone to war." The PEP program is now active in more than 100 countries and is regularly offered to people in communities who have been involved in conflict.

In Colombia, our teams have worked with ex-combatants from the FARC revolutionary group. Many of them had been fighting since they were children and knew little else. For decades, there were private armies all over the country and they were involved in terrible violence and crime, with drugs playing a big role in the chaos. Having completed PEP, an ex-fighter from the FARC said to me: "If a guerrilla can get this message to the heart, imagine what you can do for the rest of the world."

EVERYDAY CONFLICT

Talking about war can seem theoretical to those who haven't experienced it. But the exact same dynamics play out in every-day life, just in scaled-down form. Take a common example of low-level conflict. You're driving along in your car; someone cuts in front of you and they offer no apology. You're outraged! Anger floods your veins. You blast your horn and race them to the next set of lights. What's happened? You're letting them control how you feel. Where will that extra ten seconds get you? Paradise? Or just a car's length further down the highway? If you're both competing for something that's ultimately unim-portant, who's missing the point—them or you? *Both* of you!

We can try another approach. If we see somebody trying to get in front of us, we can slow down and let them in. We controlled them. Somebody's trying to take our parking spot? Let them have it. We're in control. Who knows, perhaps they have a truly urgent matter they need to attend to. Even if their need is no greater than ours, maybe our action will plant a seed of kindness in their mind.

This is important, because we see that petty disputes can quickly escalate into tragedy. Everywhere we look, people are locked in conflict, and young people in poor areas are usually at the front line. How many times do we see a news report about another young man or woman killed in a tough part of town, then just write it off as normal? When that happens, we should pause for a moment and recognize that they've lost their humanity in our eyes. They are no longer a person to us, just another crime statistic. If we stop seeing the victims of violence as human, the war in the cities will only get worse.

HOPE VERSUS BOREDOM

I'm involved in many initiatives that address youth violence, and one challenge they all face is the hopelessness people feel. Who can stop the violence? Only everyone, together. The effort begins with each one of us. The police, the politicians, the community organizations, local people, and the kids themselves—we all need to be involved. We are all human beings, and we all need to find the hope within us. You and I need to find the hope within us too.

If young people see no hope—of being connected to the community, of having a job, of having a good home, of having opportunities, of being respected and loved—they turn away from society. But even more important, they turn away from themselves. If you feel no love for yourself, why would you feel love for someone else, especially if you fear they might do you harm? These kids end up fighting with others because they're fighting with themselves.

Inside those kids there is an awful noise of boredom. Our challenge is to help them see there *is* something they can control and feel and enjoy and treasure. It lies within them. And when they're connected to that feeling of love in their heart, they can nurture how they feel about people around them. In this way, inner peace has something powerful to offer everyone.

FAMILY MATTERS

We do have to ask of the choices young people make: Why is friendship with strangers more meaningful than friendship with their family? Sometimes it feels like the family doesn't have time for the kids. Everyone seems to have so many other things demanding their attention. Sometimes the parental version of giving responsibility to the kids is to leave them to get on with their lives. Guess what: then they feel alone, and they turn to a gang for friendship. Young people can become so desperate for acceptance into that new family that they go and kill someone as an initiation test.

Governments need to support the family. Businesses need to support the family. But, most of all, *we* need to support the family. And what can we all do to empower the family? Start with our own.

A SHOCKING SMILE

Prison is the destination for many young people who are currently lost to themselves and to society, as well as for older people who can't escape the gravitational pull of offending. The PEP was originally created to help those inside prison reconnect with themselves, discover their inner resources, and feel personal peace. It can entirely change how inmates understand who they are, transforming their experience both inside and outside prison walls. The program has also proved helpful to staff at the institutions we support.

I never expected to go inside so many high-security prisons! They can be pretty sobering places to visit, but it always makes for a remarkable experience. I can't help but feel that prison is really a little replica of the world—a microcosm. Inside, you encounter every type of person.

Throughout my childhood I heard my father talk about the conversation between Krishna and Arjun on the battlefield. It wasn't until my first visit to a prison that I understood what that conversation might have sounded like. The cacophonous noise and sense of dislocation inside are something else. There's no atmosphere of peace in any prison I've entered. But when I go into those places, I often encounter what I can only describe as the most shocking form of smile: shocking because the inmates are living in utterly bleak surroundings—and may be there for many years—yet they can express such positive energy.

During one visit, I realized just how much people lose in terms of control when they end up inside. Out in the wider world they may have faced all sorts of pressures, but at least they had their home. However rundown or troubled, that was a place they considered theirs. Behind bars they've lost even that. They are the masters of nothing. The prison controls their environment and schedule, the guards have the power, and their fellow inmates can be a source of both competition and trouble. The walls, bars, and fences are unpleasant to live with, no doubt, but being locked up with individuals who are living unconscious lives must be incredibly tough. Ultimately, however awful the physical environment, it's people that make prison truly miserable for each other.

What can I say to someone in this situation? Just this: I can't get you out of here, but I can help you be free inside yourself. I tell inmates very directly: "You *can* experience peace here!" Inner peace is not to do with what you have and don't have. Sure, everyone would prefer freedom and a comfortable home over life in a cell, but peace is not out there; it's inside you.

When inmates understand this, they realize they have a choice: they can choose to connect with the peace, love, and self-respect inside themselves or not. In jail, having a choice can feel unbelievably liberating. Choice is a type of power. Inmates may feel isolated and threatened; being able to access a place that offers joy, serenity, and clarity is a lifeline. What a change that is, to realize that there *is* a place you can go where you're always number one, where you belong, where you can feel comfort, where you can experience who you really are.

Inmates sometimes speak of the way PEP connects them to all the good inside. One said to me: "Your message resonates in my heart. I am discovering my power, my love, my nature, my peace, my joy, my artistry." That smile inmates share with me says they now understand something of what self-knowledge can offer—that they're choosing peace.

WHAT CAN YOU CHANGE?

Once that heavy door slams behind them, many prisoners will blame others for their plight. Passing responsibility onto everyone else is a form of revenge, and it continues the cycle of desperation. This is not unique to prisoners, of course; people everywhere do this.

The day a prisoner starts really looking at him- or herself instead, something profound happens. They realize—perhaps for the first time—that they have more power than they thought. They finally understand that they can't change the justice system. They can't change history. But they can change *themselves*. What an epiphany!

This change from hopeless to empowered is so important because it's individuals who make up society; it's not society that makes up the individual. We make progress together one person at a time, including those in our jails. Unless the individuals within a community are strong, that community will always have weaknesses. If it's impossible for individuals to change, then society is in trouble. Time and again, in prisons across the world—and with ex-combatants, too—I see that peace is possible.

Does someone have to be open-minded to connect with my message? I don't know; perhaps it's enough that they are prepared to listen. I do know that a number of inmates came to their first PEP event because they were told they would get a pen and a pad of paper! But while they were there, they started to listen—to *really* listen—and that changed their life.

In the prisons, I see warriors who are finally starting to win the war within, and it's powerful to be in their company. PEP gives them a very simple strategy to win that inner war, and a powerful army of inner strengths prepared to fight on the side of peace. Some inmates are behind bars for life, and they know I may never come back to their prison, but they thank me because—finally—they have experienced what it is to live in peace.

FREE YOURSELF

Sometimes I leave a prison and return to the world outside, with memories of smiling inmates fresh in my mind, only to find "normal" people rather miserable. Being separated from inner peace is a terrible life sentence, whether inside or outside prison. Fears, expectations, and prejudices: they become like walls, doors, and bars. And the person who is making your life miserable within that prison is *you*. There's no possibility of parole unless you choose to make change happen for yourself. The most painful prison is the prison within. The most violent war is the war within. The most liberating forgiveness is the forgiveness within. The most powerful peace is the peace within.

Whatever your circumstances—inside or outside prison—today is the time to recognize that you create your own sense of freedom. Our life might be far from perfect, but we can all feel the perfect peace inside us *if we choose to*. Don't underestimate the scale of transformation that takes place when you connect with the real you, when you free yourself to experience inner peace.

On that point of experiencing the real you, here's a story I shared when I spoke to inmates in the Dominguez State Jail in San Antonio, Texas, a few years back. It resonated with them, and I think it has something to say when we're in danger of forgetting the power we have within us.

So, once there was a competition between the wind and the sun—who is better? The sun said: "You know, I am what I am." And the wind said: "Yes, and I think I'm better than you. Here's how we are going to resolve this: see that man walking along? He's got his jacket on and I bet, through my power, I can make him remove it."

The sun said: "Sure, do it." So the wind started to blow. And the more the wind blew, the more the guy held on to his jacket. And the wind blew even harder, and he hung on even more, and he hung on even more, and he hung on even more. And the wind tried again, but the man was gripping his jacket so tightly that the wind grew exhausted and gave up.

Then it was the sun's turn, and all the sun did was shine. And, as it shone, off came the jacket because the man was comfortable.

Whoever and wherever we are in the world, inside each one of us there is a sun waiting to shine. Let it shine.

CHAPTER 9

Love in the Moment

When I was born, I was given the name Prem. In Hindi it means "love"—a pure, unconditional form of love offered without expectation—so the theme of this chapter has long been close to my heart.

Love comes in many forms and shapes much of our life. It takes some of us to the highest and lowest points of experience, touching all of our feelings. But there are ways to think and feel about love that can help make it glorious and constant in our life, rather than a storm of pleasure and pain that descends upon us now and again.

Over the following pages I share some personal observations on love, and some wonderful lines from poets and others. As you might imagine, I'm not so interested in love as something we project onto others, or the world outside, as in how we experience love within ourselves. Each piece is a stand-alone "note." They are intended to be like moments in a conversation: starting points rather than conclusions.

LOVE NEEDS NO REASON

To *be*, love has no need of external reasons. Expectations change. Desires change. And so relationships change. But true love is always there inside us. We cannot give it to someone, and we cannot demand it is given to us. Love is a power within. A grace within. A beauty within.

LOVE IS COMPLETE IN ITSELF

How does a tree give shade? It doesn't do anything. It's just itself, and by being itself it provides cover. Does a river advertise that it can solve your thirst issues or bring you fish? No, it just flows, and people find in it what they need. Does the wind demand respect for filling the ship's sails? No, it simply goes where it goes. How can you help the ones you love? By being *you*.

LOVE IS SIMPLE

Some lines from the Indian poet Kabir:

> In the market
> I wish everyone well.
> No one is my friend.
> And no one is my enemy.

Love can be as simple as this.

LOVE IS A FIRE

If you've ever seen a yoga class, you'll know many people struggle to keep their balance. "Find your center!" instructs the teacher, and lines of people stand there wobbling on one leg. Our emotional balance can be tough to find too, but I can tell you where your center is: your heart. Your heart is your true home.

When we feel lost, it's because we have forgotten the way back home to our heart. And then we become confused. The word "focus" comes from the Latin term for hearth—the fireplace that is the heart of the home. When we feel that fire burning inside us, we know we are home; we know we are in love.

LOVE GLOWS

When the Sun and the Moon are in the right place, magic happens and the Moon glows. When we give gratitude for what we have, we glow with the love of life itself. We all have this potential within.

LOVE IS WITHIN

Here are two short pieces from the extraordinary Hindu poet-saint Lalla Ded, who lived in fourteenth-century Kashmir. She defied social convention in her search for the divine, leaving her marriage and home to become a wandering poet and singer.

I was passionate,
filled with longing,
I searched
far and wide.

But the day
that the Truthful One
found me,
I was at home.

You are the earth, the sky,
the air, the day, the night.
You are the grain,
the sandalwood paste,
the water, flowers, and all else.
What could I possibly bring
as an offering?

LOVE LIVES IN THE MOMENT

Not too long ago, while working, I was listening to a song
inspired by one of Kabir's poems. The words and the music
were so wonderful together, I just had to stop what I was
doing on the laptop and give myself to the moment. In the
poem, Kabir is saying: don't put off fulfillment to tomorrow,
feel it now. If you are thirsty, drink now. If you are hungry,
eat now.

We can only live in this moment called "now," so we can only love in the same moment. If we think about love as something only from the past or the future, we can lose it in the present. Love has no future—it is now or never. Instead, we can open our heart to the moment and encounter something divine: not the fantasy of feeling loved tomorrow, but the real experience of feeling love in our heart today.

LOVE FLOWS

Just as we can't control the tides, neither can we control the flow of love. It moves where it feels good. It feels good when it is accepted.

LOVE SINGS SWEETLY

Here is a variation on a fairy tale written by Hans Christian Andersen. The original was inspired by his unrequited love for the opera singer Jenny Lind, who became known as the Swedish Nightingale.

So, there was a king who loved the song of the nightingale. At dusk, he would open his window and a nightingale would fly down onto the ledge, sit, and sing to him. These moments inspired joy in his heart.

One day, another king sent him a mechanical nightingale. The king was delighted. "Wow!" he thought, "What a great gift. Now I don't have to wait for the nightingale each evening. All I have to do is just wind up this thing and there it is."

So he stopped opening his window, and the nightingale stopped coming.

The king was enamored of this mechanical bird. At his command it would sing, any time of day. And how pretty it was, with its decoration of gold and diamonds.

The king would instruct the bird to sing whenever he felt like it, and it always performed. More and more he required it to share its song. Yet the more it sang for him, the less satisfying he found the music. And yet still he called on the mechanical bird to sing—morning, noon, and night.

Then, one day, the mechanical nightingale broke down. It was sent to the most skilled artisans in the kingdom, but no one could fix the mechanism.

Soon the king fell sick. He dearly wanted the mechanical nightingale to sing for him. In its absence all was horribly quiet. He would lay on his bed and nothing his courtiers said would console him. Everyone in the land had a heavy heart and feared the king was going to die.

At one point the king instructed his soldiers to go out in search of the nightingale who lived in the forest, the bird who used to sing for him. But they couldn't find it.

One night, when all was silent in the castle, the king went to his window, opened it, and looked out into the forest. He so wished that the real nightingale would return. He called out, gently saying: "Nightingale, please come! I know I was wrong. You are free to come and go as you please, and that makes your song even more beautiful. You are not at my command; I am at your command. But please have mercy on me!"

That evening, just after the sun had set, he heard a fluttering outside. The nightingale flew down onto his ledge and began to sing. The king was overjoyed.

"Thank you for coming," he said to the nightingale.

"Thank you for opening the window," said the nightingale.

LOVE WHAT IS

The Stoic philosopher Epictetus said: "If you long for your son, friend, or partner when it is not given you to have him, know that you are longing for a fig in winter." This might seem rather unfeeling of Epictetus, but there is a kindness to his philosophy. Sometimes absence, loss, and rejection are so painful that we retreat into imagining things the way we want them to be. This is a form of self-protection, but pain still comes when the illusion fades.

If we can see reality clearly, we start to appreciate what *is*, not distract ourselves with what isn't. We liberate ourselves from longing for that fig in winter and, instead, love what we already have.

LOVE IS UNBREAKABLE

Mirabai, known to some as Meera, was born in the sixteenth century in India, and she loved Krishna. Many consider her a great saint. She composed moving poetry, often expressing both her feelings of deep spiritual and emotional union with her muse, the deity Krishna, and the pain of physical separation from him. Her bhajans—devotional songs—go beyond the realm of simple devotion. Written in couplets, they are songs all humanity could benefit from. For Mirabai, love is a giving, not a taking, and when true love is given, two hearts become one. She lived a remarkable life—her husband's family made several requests that she take her own life, for example—but that could take up all the remaining pages of this book. I'll just share one of her expressions of love here.

> Unbreakable, Lord,
> Is the love
> That binds me to you:
> Like a diamond,
> It breaks the hammer that strikes it.

> My heart goes into you
> As the polish goes into the gold.
> As the lotus lives in its water,
> I live in you.

Like the bird
That gazes all night
At the passing moon,
I have lost myself dwelling in you.

O my love, return.

LOVE ISN'T ALWAYS EASY

Many years ago, I went to Sardinia with my family. As I was getting out of our rental car, my son, who was just little at the time, slammed the door on my finger. I don't know whether you have experienced something similar, but it really hurt. *Really* hurt. When I looked across at my son, I saw that he was hurting too, but in a different way. His face expressed one clear thought: "Oh no, what have I done?"

I realized that, even though my finger hurt, my feelings didn't have to hurt as well. How would it help to shout about the pain and be angry with that little boy? I looked at his face and thought to myself: "I can take the suffering away from him in how I respond." So I said: "Well, I need to take a walk; why don't you come with me?"

We went for a walk together and he kept asking: "Daddy, is your finger OK?"

"Yeah, it's fine; it's fine," I said. A white lie. My hand was shaking. It was hurting so bad, but he didn't need to know that.

I have to be honest, it took an incredible—*incredible*—amount of conscious effort to do this. I could feel part of me still wanting to shout: "Why did you have to do that!"

Did it hurt any more or any less because I didn't make a big scene? No, the physical pain was the same, but the emotional pain soon went away. It's not always easy, but to consciously choose the kind option is to turn inwardly toward love.

LOVE YOURSELF FIRST

Sometimes we look to others to fill what feels like a void within. I see friends caring for everyone in their life but themselves. Some fear being alone so much, they trade their well-being to keep others happy. But unless we love ourselves, why should anyone else value our love? We must love ourselves first.

LOVE IS IN YOUR HEART

Some lines by the poet Rumi:

The minute I heard my first love story, I started looking
for you, not knowing how blind that was.

Lovers don't finally meet somewhere, they're in each
other all along.

LOVE IS REAL

Lines by the eighth-century Sufi saint Rabia al Basri, who some consider the first true saint in the Sufi tradition:

> In love, nothing exists between heart and heart.
> Speech is born out of longing,
> True description from the real taste.
> The one who tastes, knows;
> the one who explains, lies.
> How can you describe the true form of something
> In whose presence you are blotted out?
> And in whose being you still exist?
> And who lives as a sign for your journey?

LOVE BEYOND WORDS

We can be moved by what people say and write about their experiences of the heart. And the presence of love can be beautifully framed in our memory through the language we use. Think of the gentle and revealing words that come to lovers during those sometimes fragile first days of a relationship. Think of the vows taken at weddings. Think of the wise advice we pass on to children. Think of the kind words we use to celebrate family and friendship. Think of the speeches of great leaders when they connect fully with their people. Think of heartfelt eulogies at funerals.

And yet, in its purest form, love transcends language. When we go deep, deep within our self, words drift away. When we journey inside, we move into a state of being beyond time, beyond numbers, beyond images, beyond ideas, beyond definitions, beyond labels, beyond language. In this inner universe of peace we can encounter the most perfect feeling of loving and being loved.

LOVE YOUR LIFE

In every moment we are given the great opportunity to experience and appreciate the gift of existence. Right now, we can turn away from the dark to the light of gratitude, and feel life flowing through us. When we do that, we love what *is* for us. Each day, we can choose to love our breath. To love our joy. To love our clarity. We can fall in love with life.

With each breath that comes in and out, we can accept the grace of life. When that happens, our heart fills with gratitude, and that brings more love. And thus an endless cycle flows onward.

We don't choose for the breath to come, but we can choose to love each breath. And what is the effect of that choice on our body? We start to smile.

Choose to love.

CHAPTER 10

Cultivate the Divine

A man was walking along the edge of a high mountain ridge when he stumbled and fell off. He kept falling for some time until he managed to grab the branch of a small tree growing from the cliff face. Clinging on to the branch, he looked down and saw that the ground was a long, long way below. When he looked up, he saw that it would be impossible to climb back to safety because the cliff was vertical and there were no footholds. Then he started to feel the muscles in his arms tiring.

The man became desperate. His arms seemed to grow heavier and heavier, and weaker and weaker. Finally, on the verge of letting go, he shouted out: "God, please help me, I don't want to die! Help me!"

Suddenly, a booming voice came from above: "OK, as a sign of your faith, let go of the branch, then I will save you."

The man looked up the cliff face, and he looked down the cliff face at the ground below. Then he shouted: "Is there anybody else up there?"

THROWING COINS TOWARD GOD

There's a point to that joke to which I'll get later. First, I need to tell you a little about my own religious background. Growing up, I came to know something of the different Himalayan societies and religions, and how the melt waters of culture brought a range of beliefs down from the mountains, including Sufism, Buddhism, and Sikhism. At my school, we also had Roman Catholicism. But for the most part I lived in the midst of extraordinary Hindu devotion.

In fact, my mother was a staunch Hindu, but my father was free of similarly strong beliefs because he wanted to *know* rather than just believe. He had spent his life looking for— and then speaking about—wisdom. For him, it wasn't to be found in the books and it wasn't enshrined in masonry.

Every time the family left town on a trip, we would pass roadside temples. It was commonplace for people to roll down their car window and throw a coin toward God, and there were people around to collect coins and take them into the temple, although I used to suspect that some ended up in their pockets. Whenever we passed one particular temple, my mother would always throw a coin, and every time my father then said: "Why do you do this?" She would reply: "So I can go to heaven." And my father would respond: "Give *me* the money, and I'll make sure you go to heaven." But she would just roll her eyes, roll down the window, and throw out the coin, discharging her devotion.

I would be sitting in the back of the car, and as I got a little older, exchanges like this used to get me thinking. On the one hand, I could understand my mother's aspiration, but it felt increasingly like she was simply copying what everyone else did. (This is akin to the rote learning that I write about elsewhere in this book.) Anyway, isn't there something odd about *throwing* a coin at God? At least stop the car!

As you might imagine, my father's skepticism brought him into conflict with many conventional believers. One time, he went to visit a holy place and there were a lot of devoted men there, and one of the men was standing on one leg, silently praying to God. There was a sign saying that he had been standing on this leg for many weeks and hadn't spoken a word. My father went up to him and said: "Oh God, why did you give this man a second leg? He doesn't use it. And why did you give this man a mouth? He doesn't use that, either." The guy got so upset. He shouted: "How dare you say this!" And then the second leg came down.

WHAT ARE YOU?

People often quiz me about my religious beliefs. "What *are* you?" they ask. I usually reply: "First of all, I'm a human being." In fact, I'm not keen on the way people are made to define what type of believer they are. As soon as someone responds to the "What are you?" question with a big noun—Hindu, Christian, Muslim, Jew, Sikh, Buddhist, Atheist, Jain, Taoist, Shinto, Bahá'í, and so on—a cage of rigid expectations seems to fall around them. What should be a starting point for a conversation between two open minds can become a monologue from the person who asked, "What are you?" Anyway, wouldn't *"Why* are you?" be a more interesting question to ask someone?

It may be no surprise to hear that my religious sentiment is closer to my father's than my mother's. The divine is incredibly important to me—it has shaped everything in my life—but I do not feel *religious*.

Over the years, I have met many people from different spiritual traditions, and some of them have struck me as deeply thoughtful people. I know that spirituality has been a source of great joy and support to friends of mine. I've enjoyed and learned from eloquent conversations about the divine with many believers, but I don't share anyone's faith in a heaven "up there." I'm more interested in knowing the divine inside me down here.

Once, when I was in Asia, I noticed that many of the temples were on top of mountains, and I just kept wondering why. People are down here—shouldn't the temples be down here, too, so we can go to them easily?

WHO IS GREATER THAN GOD?

There are lots of witty stories from India about spiritual matters. Here's one I particularly like, from the time of Akbar and Birbal.

One day, a poet came into the court of Emperor Akbar. The poet sang and recited beautiful poetry for him, and the

Emperor became very happy, not least because the words were all about how great he was. Akbar gave the poet a jewel, so he then composed more lines, and these were even better and more praising than the earlier verses. Akbar lavished yet more jewels on the poet, and each new poem said even more wonderful things about the Emperor.

The poet found himself saying to Akbar: "You are the greatest, you are wonderful, you are so kind," and so on, until he began to worry he was going to run out of praise. Then, late that afternoon, he blurted out: "And you are greater than God!"

All around the court there was a sharp intake of breath. Until this point, the Emperor's courtiers had been saying: "Yes, yes, yes!" to each new poem because they didn't want to go against Akbar in any way. But when the poet said, "You are greater than God!" everybody stopped in dismay. They just couldn't agree with this.

Akbar looked around the court and said: "So, am I really greater than God?"

Nobody dared speak. "Yes!" would mean getting your head chopped off, and "No!" would mean getting your head chopped off.

There was silence in the room. Then people started to look at the most intelligent and witty courtier, Birbal. There was always tension between him and the other advisers because he was so smart, and they envied his relationship with the Emperor.

Finally, one of the courtiers spoke up: "Your Majesty, maybe Birbal can answer this question?"

"Good idea," replied the Emperor. "Birbal, tell me: am I truly greater than God?"

Birbal thought for a moment and then said: "May I come back to you on this tomorrow?"

The Emperor looked a little impatient, but he said: "Yes, you may."

Next day, the court reassembled and Birbal came forward. All the other courtiers were feeling smug. They were thinking: "He's had it! If he says 'Yes,' he's done for. If he says 'No,' he's done for."

"So Birbal," said the Emperor, "have you figured it out? Am I greater than God?"

"Your Majesty," said Birbal, "I don't know if you're greater than God, but there is one thing you can do that even God can't do."

The Emperor was astonished. "What? There's something *I* can do that even *God* cannot do?"

Birbal said: "If you want to kick somebody out of your kingdom you can; but if God wants to kick somebody out, where would they go?"

And so it is for all of us, within ourselves. Everyone—regardless of our beliefs, actions, and upbringing—is welcomed into the kingdom of the divine. No one is ever kicked out from there.

THE DIVINE INSIDE

If you are a spiritual person, you should be entitled to believe whatever you want to believe. I respect everyone's freedom to create a relationship with their divine, or no divine at all. My divine is the universal power that was here before us, is all around us now, and will still be here after us. Here are some words on this from the Indian poet Kabir:

> As there is oil in the sesame seed
> As there is fire in the flint
> So the divine is in you
> If you can, awaken to that.

Humans' time on Earth will end. This planet's time will end. The stars we see illuminating our sky will pass. But the formless divine will go on. All the time we are alive it moves through us, and so an incredible blessing takes place within: an energy flowing through us with each breath, enabling us to be. That is my divine.

My divine is kind, not because it grants my wishes but because it allows the universe to exist. And in that possibility there is kindness. It's not a divine that rules a heaven above the clouds, but a divine that offers a possibility of a heaven for every creature, for all existence.

My divine is beyond good or bad: it simply *is*. To truly appreciate this you have to see the divine through its own eyes—to see through the eyes of the divine within you. It has no human attributes. You are not the divine, but it is not something separate from you. When tea is put into the teapot, the tea remains tea and the pot remains a pot. The pot is not made from tea, but it holds the tea within. You are a vessel that holds the divine within.

We always have different ideas of what is good and bad for us, but we must let those fade if we're to experience the divine we hold inside. We must move from the mind into the heart. We carry assumptions and expectations in us, but to encounter the divine, not an iota of judgment can pass. The divine is something beyond pain and pleasure, beyond ideas and concepts, beyond good and bad, beyond judgment. Yet we struggle even to begin to understand what being nonjudgmental might be like.

Heaven begins for us when we let go of the judgments, the conditions, the doubts, and the concepts and we feel the simplicity of perfection. It is there for us in every breath. To appreciate all this, and to connect with the divine within, is to truly understand the context for life. Can a human being ever achieve this understanding? Can a human being ever experience the divine? It is no ordinary task. It is almost impossible. But it is *possible*.

FINDING THE DIVINE

This is a big world with many people, each of whom has their own thoughts about what this life is, what it means, and how it came into being. Thousands of civilizations have existed before us and, hopefully, there are many more civilizations to come. Each culture has its own approach to faith, but there is always an opportunity for inner peace to exist in harmony with religious belief. Religions often talk about the heaven up there, and I talk about the heaven down here. For me, this is where we find the divine.

I don't feel the need for the comfort of an afterlife, although I recognize and respect that others do. I do feel the need to connect with the infinite feeling of peace available here and now. I always want to experience the divine inside *me*, in my heart. The sixteenth-century Indian saint and poet Tulsidas wrote:

> Only the saints who know the body's heart have attained the Ultimate, O Tulsi.
> Realize this, and you've found your freedom, while teachers trapped in tradition know only the mirage in the mirror.

SEEING THE DIVINE IN YOU

For me, encountering the divine within is a truly wonderful experience that has blessed my life. I know many others who feel this way about their own experience of inner peace. But the connection can sometimes elude us. The divine may fade from sight when we are distracted by the noise outside and inside our mind. Our mind diverts us from our heart's clarity. But each of us *can* see and experience the divine when we turn inside. And that reminds me of a story—a gentle reminder that it pays to truly know ourselves and not be led by our mind's expectations.

So, high in the hills there was a village, and it was a really ancient place. There was no electricity, no technology, and very few people had ever visited. In the center was a lovely house where a woman and a man lived. It was a happy, simple household. The man had a room set aside for himself and he would go in that room every day and pray for an hour or so.

One day a traveler was passing through—a rare occasion. He really needed to cool down after a long, hot climb up the hillside, so he left his backpack outside the door of the house and went to the river nearby.

The man of the house came out, saw this peculiar backpack, and opened it up. There were clothes and some spare boots, and then he found a mirror—the first he had ever seen. He took the mirror from the bag, looked at it, and jumped backward with shock. Then he went into a deep state of bliss because, in the mirror, he finally saw the figure he had been praying to all these years. He always imagined the deity looked something like his father and now he knew it was true. The man took the mirror and put it up on the table in his room. Now that he could actually see the form of the deity he was praying to, he started to pray for hours on end, night after night.

The wife quickly noticed that her husband was spending more and more time in his room, and she became suspicious. Finally, it occurred to her that he may have found another woman and hidden her. So, one day while he was out, she quietly walked into his room. Of course, she saw the mirror— the first she had ever seen—and almost fainted. "No wonder he doesn't come out anymore!" she thought. "He is totally in love with this beautiful woman in the mirror!"

She was furious, so she picked up the mirror and took it to

the local priest. There he was, with long gray hair, a big gray beard, shining eyes, a beaming smile. She told the priest what had happened, and he listened carefully.

The priest had never seen a mirror, so he took it from her, looked at it closely, and jumped for joy. "This is the deity I have been praying to every day!" he shouted. And he went into his temple and put the mirror in the center of the altar.

When the man, the woman, and the priest look in their mirror, they don't recognize themselves—they see their beliefs. Why? Well, if you don't know yourself, you cannot see who you really are.

THE TWO MONKS

Here's another story that captures the difference between someone who lives a devoted life in an open-hearted, open-minded way and someone who carries dogma around wherever they go. As with many stories, there are lots of versions of this tale; this is the one I like.

Two monks are walking to their monastery when they come across a river. This is their only way home, and they have to cross it. There is no bridge, and they realize they're going to have to wade through the water, but the river is deep and the current is strong.

Then the monks see a beautiful woman standing by the riverbank, with tears in her eyes. One of the monks approaches her and asks: "What is the matter?"

"Well," she says, "I need to get to my village, but the river is powerful. I fear I might be swept away by the current, but I must get across."

The monk says: "No problem. I'll take you across."

He lifts her up, puts her on his shoulders, and walks her across the river. On the other side he puts her down, she thanks him, and he blesses her. The other monk follows across the river and they both walk off toward their monastery.

The monk who didn't help is silent almost all the way, until they reach the walls of the monastery. Suddenly he says: "What you did was so inappropriate! How can a *monk* put a young woman on his shoulders like that? How dare you! I thought you had renounced the world!"

The monk who had helped the woman looked at the other monk and said: "You know, I only took her on my shoulders from one side of the river to the other; you have brought her all the way to the monastery."

PRAYERS OF GRATITUDE

The joke I told at the opening of this chapter highlights the tensions that can happen when belief encounters everyday life. I know from speaking to many friends that faith can endure tough tests. Those who feel they *know* their divine, rather than just believe in it, often seem particularly resilient in the face of such questioning. The heart can be stronger than the mind in certain situations. I also entirely understand why people turn to prayer when they face difficult circumstances—in the case of the joke, when the unfortunate man is experiencing the understandable desire not to fall to his death! I just feel that we might also consider praying when things are going *well*.

For me, a true prayer is when you give thanks, not just when you make personal requests. Find a war, and you will see soldiers on both sides praying for victory. Here's a little story about prayer.

One day a young man was cycling to an important job interview when his bike ran over a sharp rock and got a puncture. "This is terrible," the man thought. "Unless I can fix this tire, I'm not going to get the job," and he started to pray for a solution to his problem. Around the next corner was another young man, sitting outside his bicycle repair shop. "This is terrible," he thought, "unless we get a customer today, I'm going to lose my business." And he began to pray.

You see, one person's misfortune can answer another person's prayer. But the deeper and more powerful form of prayer is when we simply give thanks for what is, not what might be. In my experience, you always get a response to prayers of gratitude.

When we give heartfelt thanks for the life we have been given, it is a wonderful expression of the peace inside us. The voice of our heart is ready to sing with gratitude; with the appreciation of all that is good and right in our life. Here is a delightful paradox for you: gratitude makes us feel complete, but we always have the capacity for more. We all have an infinite capacity for peace, joy, and love—isn't that remarkable?

There is a beautiful song by the eighteenth-century Indian saint Swami Brahmanand that expresses the spirit of gratitude. To *his* divine he sings these words:

It is an amazing creation you have created,
From a mere thought you have created this play
Without pen, paper or color you have created magnificence
In all I see a face, from one face you have made many
From a drop of water you have created all beings
Within all the temples of the heart you have made your home
Without pillars and beams you support this creation
Without land you have made an enchanting palace
Without seed you created an entire forest
You reside with everyone yet hidden
Brahmanand's heart is filled with immense joy
When the master shows me the hidden you.

What an eloquent appreciation of the divine inside us.

CREATING HEAVEN HERE

Whatever your beliefs, there is a heaven *here* for you on Earth right now—a heaven to treasure and enjoy in all its countless ways. What is heaven? Heaven is the place where you feel fulfilled. What does heaven feel like? It feels heavenly.

We encounter this heaven when we open our eyes and our heart to it; when we feel it in the here and now; when we acknowledge the beauty of *being*, here on this planet today. When a child is born and it weighs seven pounds, does the Earth get seven pounds heavier? No. And when the same person dies as an adult weighing two hundred pounds, does the Earth get two hundred pounds lighter? No. This is where we are—this Earth.

Here is a story that dramatizes what I am saying about heaven (and hell.)

A king has to fight a war, and he knows he will be at the very forefront of the battle. Unlike some of our political leaders, who can be quick to start a war but will never be anywhere near the fighting, this king knows he's in for a bloody time. All night long he's thinking: "I might die. And if I die, am I going to go to heaven or am I going to go to hell? But what even *is* heaven? And what *is* hell?"

All night long this goes on.

In the morning the king puts on his armor, gets on his horse—his army lined up behind him—and marches toward the battleground. All that time, part of his mind is turning over those questions: "What is heaven? What is hell?"

Then, as he's riding along, he sees a much-venerated wise man walking the other way. He gallops over to the wise man and says: "Stop! I want to ask you two questions! What is heaven? And what is hell?"

The wise man says: "I'm late. I don't have time to answer you."

The king is furious. "Do you know who I am? I am the King! You don't have time for your ruler? How can this be?" And he's getting angrier and angrier.

The wise man looks at the king and says: "King, now you are in hell."

The king takes a moment to think about this: "OK, he's right! He really is wise." He gets off his horse, gets on his knees and says: "Thank you. You opened my eyes. Thank you *so* much!"

The wise man looks at him and says: "King, now you are in heaven!"

You see, all he said was three things, but he answered the king's biggest question. Where was the curiosity about heaven and hell? In him. Where was this hell? In him. Where was this heaven? In him.

When there is confusion, anger, and fear, you are in hell. When there is clarity and gratitude, you are in heaven. This is how it is.

LIVING IN HEAVEN

When we appreciate the importance and wonder of each moment, we are getting close to understanding what immortality is. The present moment is immortal because we are always in it. We experience heaven on Earth when we live consciously in each moment, and we achieve this through being conscious that we're blessed with existence. The height of existence is to truly feel the peace within—this is *the* most heavenly experience for me.

The heaven of inner peace is an end in itself, but that

feeling of fulfillment can also make a heaven of the world around us.

When you live in peace, to see the first gentle stirrings of sunrise is heavenly.

To feel the warmth of that sun as it rises, bringing in the day and all its possibilities, is heavenly.

To hear the dawn chorus of birds, singing to their heart's delight, is heavenly.

To see the rays of the sun dance on the ocean is heavenly.

To see a whale defy gravity for a few joyful seconds is heavenly.

To smell a cloud of scents rising from a sun-warmed garden is heavenly.

To feel a fresh wind on your face is heavenly.

To drink deep of ice-cold water on a hot day is heavenly.

To eat the sweetest fruit straight from the tree is heavenly.

To see the setting sun sink gently into the horizon, bidding goodbye to the day and pointing us toward rest, is heavenly.

To know that there is always a sunrise and a sunset taking place somewhere on this beautiful Earth is heavenly.

To see the shapes of the land painted by soft moonlight is heavenly.

To hear the call of the owl in the dark forest is heavenly.

To see the stars shooting overhead, sudden and sublime, is heavenly.

To see someone you love smile is heavenly.

To feel content is heavenly.

To feel the divine in your breath is heavenly.

These feelings are the joy of life itself—not steps on the path to something else, but the pure bliss of being. They are there for all of us to savor—wherever we live, whatever our age, whatever we believe, whoever we are.

This is what it feels like to be in heaven. So, what is hell? It's when we are not in heaven.

CHAPTER 11

Become the Universal Self Through Kindness

One day in Dehra Dun, when I was twelve, I arrived home from school and noticed a strange camper van parked outside our house. It was made by Commer, a British manufacturer, so the van stood out among all the Indian-made Ambassador cars that we were used to seeing in our area. None of my family had ever left India, so the arrival of this foreign vehicle on our street was intriguing. At that time, I was a big fan of the TV show *The Twilight Zone*, which was all about sci-fi mysteries, aliens, suspense, and that sort of thing, so my imagination went into overdrive. Who might be inside the Commer van and why were they here?

I was full of curiosity as a kid, and I was pretty confident too, so I walked straight over to the van and opened its doors. Then I got a shock: the back of the vehicle was full of very pale people, sitting quietly and wearing the most extraordinary outfits. Today we'd simply think: "Hey, there are some hippies in a camper van!" but back then pretty much *everything* about these visitors was new to me. They were wearing an odd combination of Western and Indian clothes, and they all had long hair, including the men. To me this was an incredible sight. But that was nothing compared to the smell. Wafting out from the vehicle came a heavy scent of sweaty bodies, incense, and other ingredients that had obviously blended together on a very long, hot journey. I took one step back and tried to understand what my eyes and nose were reporting to me.

One guy looked at me very closely then wiggled his fingers in a sign of greeting. I think I half-waved in response, but my brain was still processing the scene. Slowly, the strangeness of the encounter gave way to a rather lovely sense of: "Okay, so there are some strangers here that are clearly very different from us, but they seem like friendly human beings."

After a few moments, I got to talking to these men and women, and it turned out they'd come to see me. They wanted to meet this kid who spoke from the heart about inner peace. Over the next few days, they asked me many questions, and I answered as best I could. As the dialogue evolved, mutual respect grew. Their questions were asked in English, but they weren't really any different from those that Indians asked me all the time.

CROSSING THE BARRIER

The Western visitors stayed for a while, and more Westerners joined them, and we started to get to know one another a little better each day. Some of the adults in and around my family were less open to crossing the cultural barrier than I was, however. They viewed the strangers as unclean, and I don't just mean unclean in the sense that they needed a good shower after living in the back of that van; I mean they were seen as spiritually unclean. At that time—the 1960s—a lot of Indians were proud that people from the West were starting to visit their country, but they were somewhat wary of them, too. Hearing about foreigners was one thing, encountering them for yourself something else entirely.

One day, an American woman from among the group of foreign visitors walked into our family kitchen to ask for some food. She was politely but firmly asked to leave, after which the entire kitchen had to be made "holy" again—which meant it had to be cleaned from top to bottom. It was as if an Untouchable—someone deemed "impure" because they were from a low-caste group, or from outside the caste system altogether—had come in. I was really shocked at the way this person had been treated. I said: "But it's just another human, and she simply walked in looking for food. Let's give her some food!" But the reply was clear: "No, this can't happen."

Something I understood clearly a few years later, when I went to South Africa, was that people who feel inferior often look for ways to assert themselves over others. Some feel that by controlling others they elevate themselves, but this is nothing more than an absurd case of ego inflation and it's always destined to fail in the end. The much better way to address a feeling of inferiority is to develop respect and love for yourself, not project negative qualities onto others. When we put ourselves first, the desire for prejudice evaporates.

The strange visitors in the Commer van—some of whom became my life-long friends—had crossed plenty of physical barriers on their journey to reach India. They'd had some pretty interesting experiences in Afghanistan and Pakistan, as you can imagine. Such a journey seems almost unthinkable right now, or at least somewhat unwise.

More and more, the Westerners started to wear dhoti (a cloth wrapped around the legs and knotted at the waist) instead of trousers, and kurta (a loose collarless shirt that stretches to the knees) instead of Western-style shirts. To be honest, I thought they looked rather funny in those local outfits, but they loved them. Back then, when I traveled for speaking events, I wore dhoti-kurta too, but every single day at school I was in a uniform of pants, jacket, Western-style shirt, and tie. So, most of the time, the Westerners were dressed Indian style and the Indian school kids were dressed Western style!

It wasn't until I traveled to England with some of my new friends that I realized how different two cultures could be. It was the first time I'd been abroad, so it was bound to feel odd, I suppose. Everything was alien to me, and I mean *everything*. I remember, soon after I arrived, the thought struck me very clearly: "I'm not in India anymore." In fact, it wasn't just the thought of it, it was a deep *feeling* of how far I was from home. That was June 1971, and what I didn't know then was that I wouldn't return to India until November.

On the day I arrived in London, I went to a house that had

been rented for me, took a bath, and then came downstairs. Sitting on a couch trying to shake off the jet lag, I was surrounded by a group of people sitting on the carpet, most of whom I'd never met before. They were looking at me and I was looking at them. Not a word was exchanged at first. And then, rather gently, we began to talk, and their welcome proved really warm.

From those first days in England I developed a strong commitment to respecting the people of the country I'm in. That's been an important thing in my life, as I've been to many, many places to share the message of peace. I bring my own culture, but I always want to respect the culture of the land I'm visiting. I travel the world, but home is now the US. As an immigrant here, I wanted to become part of the local culture and also add to it. I feel it's really important that immigrants try to get this balance right.

This issue of immigrants "getting the balance right" has been going on for centuries. When the Persians came to India looking for shelter, they encountered resistance. Some local people felt the country was already full and there were already too many demands on food and water sources. The king, receiving a party of senior Persians, called for a glass of milk to be brought to him, along with a separate small jug of milk. He showed the glass of milk to the Persians and said: "Just like this glass, we are full. Adding more will cause this country to overflow." With that, he poured some extra milk from the jug into the glass, causing the milk to overflow and spill onto the floor.

At this point, a wise Persian stepped forward and politely took the glass from the king. From his pocket he brought out some sugar and mixed it into the milk. "Now the milk is even sweeter," he said, "and none has been lost from the glass. We will add to your society, not take away."

LOOKING FOR DIFFERENCES

When I'm piloting a plane, I sometimes make an announcement along these lines: "If you look out the windows right now, you'll see the border between so-and-so country and so-and-so country just below us." Of course, I always choose a border that you can't see. People start to look really hard at the ground and then they realize there's no barrier visible at all, just a seamless stretch of mountain range or desert or fields or ocean. We're always looking for differences and division.

Try talking about borders to an ant. Some householder puts up a little picket fence outside their home, and the ant will keep going from one side to the other all day long, back and forth, back and forth. Try talking about borders to a bird. "Hey, you with the wings, where's your passport?" There are no borders for the crows, the bees, and the butterflies; no borders for the fish, the dolphins, and the squid; no borders for the clouds, the wind, and the water.

From childhood, we are taught about the differences between people, and we grow to believe in them. "We are from here, so that means we are like this and this. They are from there, so that means they are like this and this." Yet the differences between people are often just on the surface. An Indian might say: "Our food is unique: look at our wonderful chapati." An Italian might say: "Our food is unique: look at our wonderful pasta." But what is pasta made from? And what is chapatti made from? They're eating the same thing prepared in slightly different ways. Big deal!

If someone goes in for surgery on their heart, are the doctors going to perform a different operation according to the person's race? Doctors don't go through medical school learning how to treat people by their color.

We have so much more in common. "I am thirsty" can be said in many languages, but it always means one thing. I'm often asked: "Where are you from?" And I have to smile. What do I say? "I'm from the same place you are—Earth!" Sometimes the questioner looks at me as if I'm a crackpot, but I'm just speaking the truth.

When I go to Mexico, people think I'm Mexican; when I go to Malaysia, they think I'm Malay; and that happens to me in many other places too. The only place that I've actually been stopped and challenged as a suspected foreigner was India! I was going to see my sister when she was living in an area in the north. The military didn't want foreigners going in, and so, at a crossing, a soldier looked at me and asked to see my passport. I said, "But I'm Indian!" The officer came out to see what the fuss was and immediately recognized me. He laughed and turned to the soldier: "Yeah, he's Indian!"

It can be surprising the tough judgments usually open-minded people make about others *because they are different*. Once, in Argentina, I was introducing a group of people to the techniques of self-knowledge (more on that in chapter 12). One of the facilitators working with me came up and said: "There's a person here who should not receive Knowledge."

"Why not?" I asked.

"Because she has just told me she's a prostitute," he said.

I replied: "If she is a prostitute and you disapprove, don't sleep with her. What does that have to do with giving her Knowledge?"

REAL CONNECTIONS

When we step back from the ideas and concepts in our head, what does our heart tell us about our fellow human beings? It's true that you can encounter hatred in the world, as well as selfishness, envy, prejudice, and so on. Some people live their lives devoid of consciousness, and the consequences of that can harm them and others. But there are also a billion acts of kindness each day that go unreported. Generosity, creativity, gentleness, understanding—many wonderful things happen in us and around us.

Rather than being idealistic or pessimistic about human nature, we need to be realistic. The truth is that we all have good and bad in us. I have seen incredible darkness in people's eyes—seemingly bottomless darkness with no glimmer of light anywhere. And I have seen incredible light in people's eyes—a sparkling of hope, joy, and love—even in people going through rough times. We all have the potential for both darkness and light, and they live side by side within us.

All that I consider to be good in me is never far from all that I dislike. Love is never far from hate. Clarity is never far from confusion. Light is never far from darkness. All it takes is just one flick of a switch to turn light into darkness and darkness into light. We don't need to worry about removing the darkness from our life; just focus on bringing in the light. We don't need to worry about removing confusion from our life; just focus on bringing in clarity. We don't need to worry about removing the hate from our life; just focus on bringing in love.

There are many qualities within us—it's the ones we choose to act on or express that determine so much about our life. This ability to choose is a fundamental part of the human experience. Our humanity is grounded in our ability to choose.

So, once there was a man, and he was normal in every aspect except one: he thought he was a grain of wheat. This didn't really pose much of a problem until he saw chickens. When he saw a chicken, he would freak out, thinking he was going to get eaten.

This problem kept getting worse, until his family couldn't stand it anymore. Whenever they went somewhere together, he'd inevitably see chickens, and then he'd scream and run away. It didn't make for an enjoyable day out. So they took him to a doctor, who recommended a special institution. The man went to stay there, and the doctor treated him. Day after day after day she worked with him and tried to convince him that he was a human being, not a grain of wheat.

It took a long time—a really long time—but one day the doctor asked him: "What are you?" And he replied: "I'm a human being!"

"Are you sure you're a human being and not a grain of wheat?"

"Absolutely, I'm a human being!"

"You know what," said the doctor, "you're cured. You may now leave this institution."

The man was very happy because he was going to get out. The doctor signed his certificate, and he took it and left. The doctor was very relieved.

About fifteen minutes later, the man came back. The doctor was surprised: "What are you doing here? I said you could go! You're cured!"

He looked at her and said: "Doctor, I know I'm cured, but has anybody told the chickens that I'm not a grain of wheat?"

That's our problem! OK, we probably don't think we're a grain of wheat, but we can just get confused about exactly what we are. What are we? A human being! And a human being is a creature who carries in their heart an ocean of love, of kindness, of light. We all have these qualities somewhere within us. Rather than looking for what separates us, we can always choose to celebrate the wonders that live inside us all—including inside you and me.

NEEDS UNITE US

Culturally, people often seek different things. Just look at how various communities and societies approach death. The Toraja people on the Indonesian island of Sulawesi keep the mummified bodies of their dead relatives in the family home while they are saving up to pay for elaborate funerals. The bodies are kept for months and sometimes years in this way, being treated as "ill" rather than dead, and brought food and drink, and sat with and talked to. Even after they are laid to rest in a family tomb, the dead are still taken out of their coffins every so often to refresh their hair and clothes, and relatives talk to them and take photographs. To some of us, this might seem macabre. To others, this ritual is a heartfelt way of honoring and remembering loved ones who have passed.

In Mongolia and Tibet, many local people believe the human spirit lives on after death. To help the process of reincarnation, bodies are chopped into pieces and put out on a mountain top, often near a place where vultures visit. The birds are seen as angels who help the spirit ascend to heaven while it awaits its rebirth, hence the name of this tradition: "sky burial."

In most Hindu cultures, the body of the deceased is burned and there's no trace left, just a picture of that person with a garland around the frame. When you walk into someone's home and see one of those garlanded photographs, you know the person has gone but that they remain in the family's heart.

Go around the world and you will find many other ways in which the dead are remembered. I even hear you can now take cremated remains and, instead of putting them in an urn, have them made into a diamond using extreme heat and pressure, and then used to make jewelry!

So yes, there are cultural differences among people, and this is something we can often note, enjoy, and even celebrate. But these differences are just part of how we live on the face of this Earth; they do not define the very essence of what we are. Wants and desires, rules and rituals—these are really about lifestyle, not life itself. There are other things that unite us, regardless of where we are from and what we believe, not least our fundamental needs.

Needs are what we cannot do without. We all get hungry and thirsty. We all require shelter. We all share the same air that wraps around this stunning planet. We breathe in and we breathe out.

How we work together to meet our needs is always a fascinating blend of individualism and universalism. Today, when we look around the world we humans have built, what do we see? How have we responded to the challenge of meeting our shared needs? Sometimes we see such wonderful human progress, such bounty and beauty, such generosity and material benefits. Other times we see the effects of fear and greed: pollution, food shortages, health issues. Here, again, choice is key. If we can do bad things, then we can also do good. It's humans who often create awful circumstances for other humans, but there's always that possibility we can alleviate those circumstances too. And it often starts with small steps.

Take hunger. Hunger is natural, but scarcity of food is a

human-made problem. Nature can provide all the food we need and more if we work with it in the right way. Yet the distribution of food is so poor and the wastage so great. It shakes me every time to think that there are still people in India dying of malnutrition, yet India exports a lot of the food it produces.

Some years back, a team from the Prem Rawat Foundation and I went to see how we could help address some of the problems happening around Ranchi, the capital of the Indian state of Jharkhand. The area had suffered serious political tensions and communal violence, along with very high levels of poverty. Even though the land there has around 40 percent of India's mineral resources, a similar percentage of people were living below the poverty line and were malnourished.

We had found some land and were thinking of buying it so we could build a facility to help local people. Our advisers said: "Don't do it; this area has a terrible problem with terrorism and crime, and we can't assure the safety of anyone working here." But if we had given up, those same problems would just have continued. So we kept going.

The question was this: How could we have the maximum positive impact for local communities? Someone said we should build a hospital, but we had no expertise in that area. It would have been a big challenge to construct it and an even more complex job to run it. Then someone suggested we build a school, but there were already plenty of schools in the area and, again, I didn't feel we had the capacity to manage it. Then we thought about nutrition, and that really struck a chord with everyone. The situation was pretty desperate for many families. Some of the local kids I met had learned how to find and dig out rats' nests so they could steal the food waste the rodents had collected. We decided to build a large food center offering hot, nourishing food every day, for free.

I really wanted to avoid any political interference in who would be allowed to eat and who wouldn't. So we invited all the local community leaders from the region and gave them the final say on who was to receive free meals. Soon after, kids started coming, then older people and mothers with infants. As part of the development, we'd built a bathroom facility, and imposed a rule that everyone had to use it to wash their hands thoroughly. That was new to a lot of the kids. Back home, some would collect dung from the fields first thing in the morning, because it was used as fuel. They told me that they would go straight from doing that to eating breakfast, with no handwashing in between.

The food center's kitchens were, and continue to be, spotlessly clean. All the people working in them wear masks, the food—delicious and locally sourced—is carefully prepared, and everyone who visits can eat as much as they want.

After a few years we saw the impact of our food-centered approach, and it was unbelievable. Crime went down because people had more money, having made savings from their family's food budget. That extra money also meant fewer fathers left to find employment far away, and that fewer kids were spending all day working. The kids started to attend schools in much higher numbers and they began to graduate, too. Child health improved, so pressure on local hospitals decreased. And because they could see that what we were doing was helping local people, local terrorist groups left our teams and equipment alone.

Even now, I can't quite believe that just one good meal a day can make so much difference to an entire area. We've now put in place something similar in Ghana and Nepal, programs that have also had a big positive impact. Once again, small steps are creating big change.

(An aside: our center in Nepal was properly constructed, following the building code. When the big earthquake hit in 2015, many of the nearby buildings collapsed or became unsafe, but ours just had a little crack, so it became a shelter too. So the center *really* became a lifesaver.)

ON KINDNESS

Here's a little joke about an entirely different way we human beings sometimes respond to other people's needs.

There's a man lost in the desert and he's really thirsty. He's on his hands and knees, crawling and crawling, and his tongue feels like it's made of sand. He's *so* thirsty. Then he comes across this guy on a camel. He says to the man: "Please, please, please can I have some water?"

"Well, how about I give you a tie?" says the man. And, sure enough, he undoes his side pack, and there are all these neckties in it. "Which tie would you like?" he asks.

"No, no, I don't want a tie," says the thirsty man. "Do you have any water?"

"Well, how about a tie?"

"No, I don't want a tie," says the man, and he keeps crawling. Then he looks back and says: "Are you sure you can't tell me where there is some water?"

"Oh, yeah, I can tell you where there's some water. Just go straight for about a half a mile and you'll come across an oasis and there's water there. Plenty of water."

So the man is crawling on his hands and knees, and he finally gets to this beautiful oasis. There are gorgeous trees, plants, and flowers, and he can see a deep pool of water shimmering behind all the greenery. A big guy is standing in his way on the path to the oasis, so the thirsty man crawls up to him.

"Can I come into the oasis and drink the water?" he says.

"Well, are you wearing a tie?"

That's what we end up doing if we're not thinking consciously—we make people jump through our hoops before they can satisfy their needs. Instead, what if we treat people the way we'd like to be treated? What if we look for common purpose rather than competitive differences? What if we are simply *kind*?

The word "kind" has a shared history with "kin," meaning one's family and relations. When we think and act with kindness, we break down the barriers between *us* and *them*. We can give of kindness to every single person we meet, and we would be missing nothing and gaining everything. And we could multiply that seven billion times, and nothing would be lost and everything would be gained.

When we spread kindness, we create a family of those we connect with. And then we have a kindred spirit: we feel we are one. But to share kindness outwardly requires that, first, we must be kind to ourselves. Kindness starts with our own self—a connection fostered with the best human qualities inside us—and it springs from there.

Empathy has long, long been part of human experience, but the word was only coined in the twentieth century. There are now many definitions of it, but I just want to point to the power of empathy in its simplest sense: putting yourself in the other person's shoes. You might not be able to share the same experience, and you might not agree with them, but it's important to try to understand where that person is coming from. This is a far better way to understand the world around you than always seeing others as entirely separate from you. Instead of starting by trying to categorize the person—by religion, or color, or nationality, or whatever—you simply try to place yourself within whatever they might be feeling. From hunger to pain to misery to anger to war, you just have to try to empathize with people whose needs are not being met. To do this is to remember what it is to be human.

SOCIETY AND THE SELF

Kindness starts from within, so if we want to make the world a better place, we should first look to ourselves. I've been around the world a few times and I haven't encountered a perfect society yet. What I've seen is that getting an entire society to change is tough. It takes time. Sometimes we progress, sometimes we regress. If we start with ourselves, we may well be able to change what *we* think and how *we* act, and *then* we can act collectively.

The condition of each brick determines the strength of a building. If one brick is cracking and crumbling, it affects those around it. And the effect is passed on, putting each neighboring brick under more pressure. When the safety of a building is assessed, the individual integrity of each brick must be considered. And it's the same with the individual and society. We need to take care of each unit, and that really starts with each person trying to make themselves as strong as they can be.

Think of a watch. Inside there are many, many, many parts. Some move, some don't, but in a good watch they will all be essential. On the outside you only see an hour hand, a minute hand, a second hand, but inside there is an entire little world. All the parts join to put that hour hand in the right place, and that minute hand, and that second hand too. Watchmakers know that for this to happen accurately, day after day, each part must be functioning properly.

Here's another way to look at this. You're in front of the TV and you see a picture of the world from space, then you start zooming in, zooming in, zooming in, zooming in. Now you're looking at a picture of mountains, then a forest on the side of one mountain, then a small number of trees, then leaves on one tree. And you keep zooming in, zooming in, zooming in. The picture of leaves has quickly turned into blobs of color, and you keep zooming in, zooming in, zooming in until you end up looking at three rectangles: one red, one green, and one blue. You've reached the level of a single pixel. That's what you've been looking at all along, but what you actually *saw* was a picture of a leaf, and a tree, and a mountain, and an entire world.

Each human being is like one pixel, and together we form a community, then a society, then a global population. If the big picture of society looks wrong, we need to be asking what's wrong with the pixels—why aren't they lighting up in the right way? And what about *me*; am I helping build a good picture of my community, society, and world? Am I lighting up in the right way? What happens when we zoom into our self?

It takes just one broken part to stop a watch, to weaken a building, to corrupt a clear picture, to disrupt society. And this is why it is never selfish for us to spend time understanding ourselves. To illuminate an entire world, you start with one lit candle.

WE ARE FROM THE SAME PLACE

Looked at from a certain perspective, "The Universal Self" may seem like a paradox. Isn't a "self" something distinct from everything else? Am I not uniquely *me*? Are you not uniquely *you*?

Yes, for the time we're alive, there is something distinctive about each of us, but we all share the same set of fundamental needs, including the need for peace in our heart. Inner peace is not reserved for the powerful or the weak, for rich or poor, for one race and not another. Peace is there for everyone and inside everyone.

Our minds constantly *work* at trying to shape the world around us, but existence is beautifully simple. Think about when we're asleep: What is the difference between rich and poor then? Between educated and uneducated? Between good and bad? In sleep our concepts and differences drift away, and we simply breathe.

We share a set of fundamental needs and we share this planet, but we also share something greater still: our ever-expanding universe. A line on a map seems pretty insignificant when we imagine the vastness of space. That is the true nature of our home. Here's something the French philosopher Simone Weil said on this subject:

> We should identify ourselves with the universe itself. Everything that is less than the universe is subject to suffering.

The divine spark of universal power is in us from the moment we are created, and it forms an invisible web of connection between everyone and everything. We are simultaneously different and the same. We are one.

Dogma may divide us, but the divine within unites. Not everyone is conscious of this link from person to person, friend to friend, stranger to stranger, yet it can burst into view at any time, like the sun reappearing after a storm. The Indian poet Kabir expressed our universalism in these words:

We all know that there is a drop in the ocean, but very few know that there is an ocean in the drop.

There's that paradox again: the ocean in the drop. For a moment, let's go with Kabir's flow and imagine humankind as water, moving together as one in the ocean. Then see that each and every drop is lifted from the waves, carried by clouds and let fall onto different places—the hills, the plains, the towns—before flowing back toward the starting point of the journey. Along the way, the drops join together to become streams and grow to become mighty rivers with names and histories. The Mississippi, Amazon, Ganges, Thames, and all the rest join to form seas, and then all the seas join together to become one vast, nameless ocean that spans the Earth. Is that the end of the journey? No, it starts over: drops of water are drawn up from the waves . . . and on it goes. And so *our* journey goes. We are both one drop and one ocean.

The Earth has been recycling its water for billions of years. The constant beginning and end of water are like the alpha and omega of the never-ending divine: the process never stops. By the way, I'm not making a case for reincarnation! I'm saying that the divine was there before us, is busy animating us throughout our life, and will be there after us.

Recently, someone asked me, "How's it going?" and I

replied "Well, it's going. That which supports the nature of going is busy going, and that which supports the nature of coming is busy coming. All that comes goes one day, but the nature of the divine is to be present always. This is the only constant." I don't think they were expecting that reply!

Our human form is one passing expression of that ever-flowing cycle of life. Ultimately, we are all at one with each other, with the universe, and with the divine. This is the universal self.

CHAPTER 12

Practice, Practice, Practice

Think of life as a book. The front cover is opened when we are born. Inside we find the acknowledgments and preface: our early childhood. We can't claim much credit for this part, but soon the story really gets going. As each new page is turned, we have the opportunity to write something, every day putting fresh ink on the blank white paper of our existence.

If you're fortunate, there will be many pages in your book, the story rich with your adventures and experiences. As with all stories, there will also be some rough times along the way. Then, one day, all the pages but one will be written, and on that final page two words will appear: "The End."

What are you writing in *your* book? Does it make sense? Does it hold your attention? Does it inspire you? Is it the story you want to tell?

According to ancient Indian history, when the legendary sage Ved Vyās wanted to compose the *Mahabharat*, he needed someone sublimely clever to capture his spoken narration on the page. He needed a writer. So he turned to Ganesh, the revered god of wisdom. Ganesh said that he would write as long as his pen did not stop flowing. Ganesh was really saying to Ved Vyās, "I want you to speak from your heart and not overthink this." In turn, Ved Vyās asked of Ganesh that he write down "only what makes sense to you." Whatever you write in the story of your life, it too must make sense to you. Is what you're writing your story or someone else's? Does it have clarity and purpose? Does it have meaning for you?

Every day brings a new opportunity for us to express ourselves—a new blank page waiting to be filled. Self-knowledge can help us write something memorable, something joyful, something true to who we really are. Something full of meaning. Only I can write the story of *my* life and only you can write *yours*. Each day we need to pick up our pen and write what is in our heart. Let the ink flow.

I know it's not always easy to do this. I understand that the journey from feeling distracted and discontented to experiencing inner peace and a fulfilling life isn't always straightforward. Sometimes we can feel our story is being drowned out by the world of noise. On occasions, I find all this difficult too. It requires practice. If we want to row our boat down the river, we don't just pull on the oars once or twice.

In this chapter, I'm going to talk a little more about the challenges we face on the path to inner peace, and what can help us. I'll express again why all this is so important in our lives. And, along the way, I'm going to talk about how we are all on vacation from being dust. Yes, dust. As ever, rather than tell you what to think, I'm hoping the words that follow offer further ways we can understand and connect with ourselves a little more.

WHERE WE HAVE BEEN

If you've traveled with me from the Introduction onward, we have covered a lot of ground together. We've explored how the busyness of modern life creates noise all around us, but it's the noise between our ears that most affects how we live. We've considered how life is so very precious, and that by connecting to the peace inside us we can transform our lived experience. We've looked at the difference between knowing and believing, and the value that comes when you start with yourself rather than expect the outside world to meet your needs. We've seen how our life can blossom through gratitude, and how inner peace can help us navigate through the rough times and the wars within. We've heard songs of love, celebrated the heaven that is to be found here on Earth, and felt our universal connections.

Throughout this book, I've repeated the message that peace is always there inside us and is *knowable*, and I've done that with good reason. The simplicity of this insight is key, yet our restless mind can cloud and complicate it, separating us from the clarity of inner peace. Each day there are many changeable things that demand our attention—one moment they're making us feel happy, the next they're bringing problems—but inner peace is unchangeable. Life can become all about the evolving nature of what's outside us, but personal peace is not about the outside at all. Whoever we are, wherever we live, whatever we have done, whatever change brings to us: peace is constantly there within us and, through self-knowledge, available *for us*.

Gaining knowledge about the self is a process of discovery, of uncovering who we are. What's at stake when we allow our inner self to stay hidden—when we live unconsciously? Well, we forsake the most precious thing we have: our experience of life itself. We can also suffer all sorts of mental and emotional pain. And we might also project our pain onto those we love, and on the world around us.

Self-knowledge connects us with the opposite of this: all that is good in us. Peace is the clarity in us. Peace is the understanding in us. Peace is the serenity in us. Peace is the kindness in us. Peace is the gentleness in us. Peace is the light in us. Peace is the joy in us. Peace is the gratitude in us. Peace is the beauty in us. Peace is the coming and going of this breath in us. Peace is the divine in us. Peace is all this and more. Peace brings everything that is good together in one heartfelt, timeless experience of who we truly are.

ACCEPTING PEACE TAKES COURAGE

Allowing self-knowledge into your life can bring challenges. For some, it requires that they go against the flow of their social or professional situation. Family, friends, and colleagues can be suspicious and dismissive. We can find ourselves surrounded by those who believe there's nothing to the inner world, and they're often keen to keep sharing that opinion with us.

People sometimes have a powerful voice in their head telling them not to look within, and often that's the noise of the ideas they've inherited from others. The heart says: "Please, please, please see me, appreciate me, enjoy me!" And the mind says: "No, no, no!" Then the self is divided.

Great pleasure and progress can come from our interaction with the world, but it's only one part of who we are. For someone to say, "There are two worlds—outer and inner—and they *both* matter to me . . ."—well, that requires courage. It takes a brave person to say, "My mind and my heart can be at peace with each other."

People sometimes think that if they want to experience inner peace and fulfillment, they have to withdraw to their version of a monastery or some other retreat. In their mind, it's as if there's a huge electricity generator in that remote place, and they can only power the lights of clarity and contentment when they're near that power source. Perhaps they feel that if they wander too far from the power generator, they'll find themselves back in darkness. I see it differently. As a human being, your peace, clarity, and goodness emanate from your heart. You have an inner power generator, an inner source of light, an inner sanctuary of calm—and you take all this with you wherever you go.

I sometimes fly over the Sahara Desert, and on one of these trips this analogy came to mind: Imagine you have to travel across a desert and you've brought a large bottle of water, some food, and an umbrella for shade—ample supplies for your journey. So you're in this vast landscape of sand, sand, and more sand. There's no oasis anywhere, and it's very hot and dry. Now think of this as the journey through life. Having personal peace within is like carrying the essentials of water, food, and shade with you every step of the way. Many people travel through their life empty-handed and try to convert the desert into what they need. But have you ever tried to turn hot sand into cool water? Reality is simple, but changing it is hard.

Think about the thirst you would have if you walked across the desert without water. Really sense that thirst: I'll be coming back to it in a minute.

HOW CAN I HELP?

People often ask me: "If I do this, this, and this, will I then have peace?" They're thinking they need to create it through actions, but all they really need to do is open up to what's already there within them. Understanding how to connect with that place of peace inside and feeling gratitude for it: this is called Knowledge, and it's something we can all learn. What is learning? It's experiencing the gift of life in a new way.

Some people can take the journey of self-knowledge alone; others benefit from guidance. There are many teachers and speakers in this world; if you need a little guidance now and then, find the person or people who feel right for you. Having someone there with you—someone who truly understands the self—can be reassuring. They can point the way in the dark.

This is how I see my role. It's not my place to tell people what they should or should not be; I'm here to offer reminders that we're blessed by the miracle of existence, and to help point the way toward inner peace. Only you can decide if that's the direction you want to go. Only you can decide if this is the route you want to take to get there.

Do you ever listen to Indian classical music? It's quite different from classical music in the West. It features instruments like the sitar, tabla percussion, and the bansuri (a type of flute). But there's another important instrument that doesn't get talked about much: it's called the tanpura. It has a long neck with strings that the player will pluck constantly. The person who plays it is often in the background. In fact, sometimes the tanpura isn't even given a microphone. While the other players create the raga, or melodic textures, the tanpura produces a constant harmonic drone. All the other instruments relate what they're playing back to the sound of the tanpura, so it keeps them in the right key. And the tanpura also lays down a subtle rhythm—a momentum that underpins the music, allowing the other instruments to dance around the beat.

Why am I describing the role of the tanpura? Because I think it's similar to what I do. A good teacher doesn't try to sing your song for you, or perform your instrument for you, or lay down the rhythms of your life. You play your raga, you set your own rhythm: I'm just here to help you stay in key and feel the inner momentum of the music of life. I can help you hear yourself.

My father, Shri Hans Ji Maharaj, once expressed the role of the teacher of self-knowledge through a wonderful metaphor. He talks about the Master, which is what people often call their main teacher, especially in India. Here's what he said:

Knowledge, they say, is like the sandalwood tree, and the Master like a breeze. The entire sandalwood tree is filled with fragrance, but even if it wanted to give its fragrance away, it could not. Yet, when the breeze blows, it carries the fragrance to the whole forest. As a result, other trees become as fragrant as the sandalwood tree. In the same way, the entire world could be fragrant with Knowledge.

LEARNING TO FEEL

I learned about self-knowledge at the feet of my father, quite literally. When I was a child, I would sit on the stage when he spoke, and I'd listen to what he was saying and to the questions people asked. That's how I came to understand that we are born with everything we need to experience peace, but the busyness of everyday life can obscure those strengths within. By finding our inner clarity we can start to let go of what we are not, and to clearly see what we are. It's about allowing what we don't need in our life to just fall away. What don't we need? Let's start with outdated expectations, fears, prejudices, and rules.

Over the years, I have learned that understanding cannot be put *into* somebody; we must accept it for ourselves. To do that, we need to be open to what's new. If you have an empty water glass and a bottle containing water, you must place the bottle above the glass and let gravity draw down the water. Water cannot flow upward into an empty glass. Knowledge cannot flow from an open heart into a closed mind.

Often, people will want to question everything about self-knowledge with their head. Exactly how does it work? How can I be sure it's working for me? What is the proof? In other aspects of our life, smart questions like this can be helpful, but you can only really learn about your self through experience, not theory. What *feels* right to you? What *resonates* with you? The proof is in how *you* experience it. Often our mind doesn't want to relinquish control, but it's our mind that gets in the way of us deeply feeling who we really are. Sometimes we need to let go of thinking—there's a time for believing and a time for *knowing*.

I want to tell you about a time when I experienced the difference between believing and knowing. Years ago, I was learning to ski, and I found it difficult. I could see people—even small kids—whizzing all over the mountain. They looked amazing, moving along superfast yet carving out elegant snow trails as they went. An instructor from Switzerland offered to teach me. So I put on my skis, and the first thing he said was: "Walk like this."

"That's not what they're doing!" I said. "I want to do what they're doing. Are you teaching me something different?"

"This is how you start," he said.

I resisted for a while, and then I said to myself: "OK, just let him teach. If it starts to make sense, continue. If not, think again."

At first, if I tried to go left, I would end up going right. If I wanted to stop, I would sometimes speed up. Skiing can feel counterintuitive when you're a beginner. Done right, leaning forward gives you stability, but for a while your brain keeps shouting: "Lean back!" Similarly, leaning out helps you turn, but it often seems natural to lean in. And you keep watching the front of your skis instead of where you're going!

I noticed that the instructor kept asking me: "What do you *feel*? How does it *feel*? Can you *feel* this?"

To be honest, a lot of the time what I felt was out of control. I was confused about what I needed to do. But I kept going because when you're learning, you need to accept uncertainty and move through it. And then I started to *feel* it. I stopped overthinking how to turn and let myself do what the teacher had described. The more I trusted the new feeling, the better I got.

Gaining self-knowledge is similar. People often need a little help to understand how to begin and move through uncertainty.

THE TECHNIQUES OF KNOWLEDGE

Peace is possible for everyone. To help people discover their inner potential for personal peace, I offer a free educational program called Peace Education and Knowledge—or PEAK for short. You can find out how to access PEAK at my website, www.premrawat.com. It helps you feel the strengths that are inside you, and it covers many of the themes you'll have already encountered in this book and others. Please feel free to use those free resources and send me any questions you have.

If this book and the PEAK program resonate with you, there's also an option to learn some practical but powerful techniques of self-knowledge. These should help you tap into your inner strengths and take your focus from the outside to the inside. It's these techniques that my father taught me on that day, back in Dehra Dun, when I was six years old, as I described in the Introduction. In my experience, the techniques are best passed on from person to person. They are something precious that should be learned from someone who truly understands them. (By the way, if you've read the previous eleven chapters and they spoke to your heart, you're already well on your way toward a good understanding of Knowledge.)

The key that unlocks the door to a deeper sense of consciousness is your thirst for self-knowledge. That's the thirst I mentioned earlier. Unless you feel that thirst, PEAK and any other approach may prove fruitless. If you do truly want and need to know your self, then PEAK will likely make complete sense. It's like learning a language: you must have that curiosity and drive to begin with, then follow up with the determination to practice. Knowledge is the language of the self.

FROM EXPECTATION TO EXPERIENCE

In this book, I've talked about the problem of expectations in our life. There are often great expectations attached to gaining self-knowledge and peace, too. "When I have peace, this is what it should feel like. When you have peace, this is how you should act." So go the expectations. I suggest a different approach: feel your thirst, explore self-knowledge, and allow whatever happens next to unfold naturally. It's better to relinquish any fixed ideas we have about inner peace: our expectations will just get in the way of our experience.

A while back, I was in Sri Lanka to speak, and the master of ceremonies for the event introduced herself to me backstage: "Good to meet you, but I was expecting a man who's floating a foot above the carpet!" She had an expectation of how someone connected with inner peace looks. Well, I'm not like that. Do I have peace *all* the time? No! Do I have problems now and then? Yes! Do I have extraordinary experiences of the world within me? Absolutely! Have I ever floated a foot above the carpet? Not yet!

Once, I was having a meeting with people who were pursuing the path of self-knowledge. During the question-and-answer session, a lady raised her hand and said: "I now know the techniques of Knowledge, but I don't experience anything." Everyone's ears pricked up at this. I replied: "OK, if nothing is happening, don't practice." And then she said: "Oh no, no, no! I don't want to stop, because I feel a lot of peace and I feel a lot of joy. It's really, really beautiful." The problem was that she kept thinking about what she *might* feel, rather than simply feeling what *is*. Expectations!

Somebody once said: "We don't need wings to fly; all we need is for those chains that bind us to be cut." If we cut the chains of expectation, we're free to explore, experience, and understand our self. It's in the gratitude for what *is* that knowing starts, and our practice of that can keep evolving until our very last breath.

MY EXPERIENCE OF PEACE

Having a strong connection to inner peace has been an incredible blessing in my life—through the good times and the rough times. For me, it doesn't matter what problems I have or what's happening in the world; when I cross that threshold and connect fully with my self, all concerns vaporize. And this is the possibility for every human being: to be in that place where their heart sings and they simply enjoy the music of *being*.

I often speak about the clarity that comes from self-knowledge because it can transform how we feel about ourselves and how we encounter life. Here's an analogy. When you fly an airplane, you use your senses to tell you how it's going, like keeping straight and level by watching where the horizon is. Basically, you're flying by the seat of your pants. But it's easy to become disoriented in the air, especially when weather conditions are against you or it's dark. Your concepts and interpretations of reality can be wrong. Instruments give you a whole other system to add to your senses. They tell you exactly how straight and level you are, what speed you're doing, how sharply you're turning, and so on. As a flight instructor, I can tell you it often takes time for pilots to learn to fly with instruments, partly because—like learning to ski—you have to learn to trust the expert!

Self-knowledge can enable you to develop a set of inner instruments connected to your true self. And that's where you find your reality. That's where you get to truly orient yourself.

To continue the flying analogy, cockpits have ended up having a lot of lights, so a manufacturer invented something called the "dark cockpit" concept. This minimizes which lights are illuminated, and that helps the pilot prioritize. If there's no light, everything is OK; if a light comes on, you address the cause. Compare the clarity of that to the way a busy mind keeps scanning the outside world, always on the lookout for both problems and peace.

Like anyone, I have to be aware that my mind can get in the way of my heart, and expectations can affect me too, of course. Once, in Japan, I was invited to a temple by a professor, and he was a widely respected expert on gardening. It was a very beautiful temple with magnificent gardens. We went into the grounds and sat down, and everyone was commenting on how peaceful it was. Of course, my mental gears were turning: "This is not peace," I thought, "this is quietness!"

I just sat there and started to listen—really listen—and I realized it wasn't very quiet at all. The water was running rather noisily. Then, all of a sudden, I could hear crickets, and they were all going at it! I could hear leaves rustling in the wind and birds singing. It wasn't quiet, but after a while I felt that there was a fabulous harmony to the sounds. I let the intellectual definitions of "quiet" and "peace" fall away, and I just experienced—in that moment—the song of the garden: the harmony of a beautiful reality.

ARE YOU ENJOYING THIS VACATION CALLED LIFE?

Why is the pursuit of self-knowledge so very important? Let's think once again about the wonder of our existence.

Many saints and poets have said that when we die, we go home, that this world is a place we visit. Whether you believe there is an afterlife or not, there is something sublime in the idea that we're just visiting here. I've thought a *lot* about this, and a conclusion I've reached is that we humans too easily forget where we've come from: dust. We were part of the great cosmological dust cloud before we were born, and we will go back to dust after we die. "Dust to dust," as the Christian *Book of Common Prayer* expresses it. I have written a few short lines on this theme:

ONE

The dust beneath my feet
Of fools and sages
Mixed together by the mill of time
The prince and the pauper
The saint and the robber
Ground in Earth's lot
Beggar's bowl and King's crown
Rusted into the same land
Carried by the same wind
Scattered without grace
The history of all things
Dust beneath my feet.

It's thought our universe was born a little less than 14 billion years ago, and that this Earth has been in its present form for some 4.5 billion years. *Homo sapiens* have been around for about 300,000 years. And modern humans have taken shape over the last 10,000 years—since the last Ice Age. That means humans—in the form we recognize today—have only been here for a tiny fraction of the time that Earth has existed, and an even smaller fraction of the time in the life of the entire universe. For billions of years, we were floating around in the galaxy as dust particles. Then the great universal energy acted upon us, and we were given the opportunity to live *this life* here on *this planet*, for a flash of a moment in the long history of time.

So, we have been given a vacation from being dust, and that vacation begins when we're born and ends when we die. Every plant and creature alive are on vacation. And what a wonderful destination we've all been brought to. But do we *know* we are on this fabulous vacation? Are we getting the most from our time? Are we distracted from experiencing this life? Are we savoring all we can of this precious moment—this opportunity to experience a trillion different things before we return to being dust?

Sometimes I forget I'm on vacation. Each day I want to remind myself that the most important thing for me is to appreciate this time, this opportunity, this beauty: to enjoy it and make the most of each moment. In each of those moments there is the possibility for us to feel our connection to everything else—to experience the universal self we encountered in chapter 11.

The same cosmic dust that formed us also built every planet in our solar system. We are each part of the Milky Way above and of the dirt below our feet. We are connected to the trees, and to the birds that fly in and out of their branches. To the butterfly fluttering around the flower. To the fish darting among the rushes in the glistening river. To the sunshine and the rain. We will always be part of matter, but for this short time we have also been blessed with consciousness. We were given the temporary ability to feel and to understand, so the question is this: Are we enjoying our vacation?

CARPE DIEM

The Earth, when it finally disintegrates, will fly across the universe as dust and become countless other somethings, somewhere else. This is the constant renewal of universal creativity. And so the opportunity for us is to keep connecting with now—not the yesterday that has gone, nor the tomorrow that never comes, but the miracle of our existence in this moment, and this moment, and this moment, and this moment, and so on. Yet, we often find such simple appreciation rather difficult. The Chinese philosopher Lao Tzu expressed it like this:

> Each moment is fragile and fleeting.
> The moment of the past cannot be kept, however beautiful.
> The moment of the present cannot be held, however enjoyable.
> The moment of the future cannot be caught, however desirable.
> But the mind is desperate to fix the river in place:
> Possessed by ideas of the past, preoccupied with images of
>   the future, it overlooks the plain truth of the moment.

What is the plain truth of this moment? Wisdom isn't realizing the preciousness of something when it's gone; wisdom is recognizing the preciousness of what we have right now.

What do we all have now? The possibility to experience the wonder of *being*. The possibility to see clearly what is most important in our life. The possibility to truly know who we are. The possibility to turn away from the noise and experience the peace within. Our heart is always knocking on the door of our mind, reminding us of the possibility to be at one with all that is good in us.

Imagine a food market—inside you will find the very finest edible products the world can offer: the freshest fruit and vegetables, the greatest cooked meats and fish, wonderful cheeses, the most delicious sweet things known to humankind, and the most refreshing drinks flowing from a hundred fountains. You are told that you can have anything you want from this market, but there is one condition: you can't take it with you. What would your response be? Would you be disappointed? Or would you think, "I'm going to enjoy every single thing I can while I'm here"?

Sounds familiar, right? We can enjoy so much, but we can't take it with us. *Carpe diem.*

GOOD WOLF, BAD WOLF

That brings us back to a vital point that flows through this book and is essential in the practice of self-knowledge—*choice*. In every moment we have a choice, and it is this: Do we give attention to the good in us or the bad in us? To the positive or the negative?

There was a group of Native American Indians, and one day a little boy from the tribe came to the Chief and said: "Chief, I have a question: Why are some people good some of the time but bad at other times?"

The Chief said: "That's because we have two wolves inside us, fighting each other. There's a good wolf and a bad wolf."

So the boy thought about this for a little while, then he said: "Chief, which wolf wins?"

The Chief replied: "The one you feed."

There's no need to keep punishing our bad wolf—that doesn't help the good in us. Nourish the good wolf instead: give it time, awareness, understanding, care, love. What happens then? The good wolf gets stronger.

Hatred, anger, fear, confusion—they feed the bad wolf.

Love, joy, calm, clarity—they feed the good wolf.

And so we must ask ourselves: What are we choosing today? Do we choose to encourage prejudice or understanding? Do we choose to encourage confusion or clarity? Do we choose to encourage war or peace?

Here are some lines I once read, long ago, on how our choices define us—words that have stayed with me to this day:

If you want to be strong, be gentle.
If you want to be powerful, be kind.
If you want to be rich, be generous.
If you want to be smart, be simple.
If you want to be free, be yourself.

CHOOSING TO BE FREE

Once, when I was talking to people who were learning the techniques of Knowledge, a man said: "I feel afraid."

"Afraid of what?" I replied.

"I can't let go: I can't go into this feeling."

"Why?" I said. "You are only turning inside. Don't be afraid of yourself. Fly!"

Later he came back to see me and said that the conversation had been so powerful for him because he did then let go and he *did* allow himself to fly. I asked him what that felt like. He said it was as if there was no limit to how free he could feel. No limit!

Our nature is to be free. What binds us might not be that great after all. But we must connect with the need within. Can you feel that need for freedom inside you? Can you free yourself to look through the eyes of the divine within?

When I was growing up, I learned a lesson about freedom from birds. If you take a bird that's been free and put it in a cage, it will fight to get out. But do you know what will happen eventually, if you wait long enough? It will learn to live in that cage. One day, if you open the door of the cage, guess what? The bird won't even try to fly out. I know because I once tried to release some birds that had been kept in a cage, and they didn't move. They had forgotten what freedom means. And the same thing can happen to us.

Whatever is happening in our life, we are always free to

connect with the deeper reality of who we are—to be free from being controlled by what's going on *out there*—but we must choose this for ourselves. As the rhythm of our breath rises and falls, it brings the miracle of life to us. Turn within, and in each moment you can choose to connect with the infinite peace inside you. Turn within, and you can fly far within yourself. Turn within, and the noise of the world settles into silence, enabling you to listen to the divine music of now. Turn within, and you will hear yourself. Begin!

ABOUT THE AUTHOR

Born in India in 1957, Prem Rawat brings over fifty years of experience from his extraordinary journey through life. From boy prodigy and '70s teenage icon to global peace ambassador, Prem has given exceptional clarity, inspiration, and deep life learning to millions.

Now based in the United States, and founder of the Prem Rawat Foundation, Prem works with people from all walks of life, showing them how to experience the source of peace within themselves. His global effort spans over one hundred countries, providing a practical message of hope, happiness, and peace to all, one person at a time.

He is the internationally bestselling author of *Peace Is Possible* and is also a pilot—with over 14,500 hours of experience—a photographer, classic car restorer, and father to four children and grandfather of four.